Emily Post on Etiquette

You might need
this book now.
Doing things properly
never hurts.
I will be testing
your skills when I
get back from New York.

All my love Louie,
monster.
XXX

Also in this series

Emily Post on Business Etiquette

Emily Post on Entertaining, Revised Edition

Emily Post on Guests and Hosts

Emily Post on Invitations and Letters

Emily Post on Second Weddings

Emily Post on Weddings, Revised Edition

Emily Post on Entertaining

EMILY POST

on

Etiquette

Revised Edition

Elizabeth L. Post

HarperPerennial
A Division of HarperCollinsPublishers

HarperCollins books may be purchased for educational, business, or sales promotional use. For information please write to
Special Markets Department, HarperCollins Publishers, Inc.,
10 East 53rd Street, New York, New York 10022.

FIRST EDITION

Designed by C. Linda Dingler

ISBN 0-06-274011-3

99 00 ❖/OPM15 14 13 12

Contents

Introduction   ix

Relationships   1

Getting Along with Others   13

Meeting and Greeting   32

Communications   43

On the Job   55

Table Manners   67

In Houses of Worship   100

At Times of Loss and Grieving   106

Invitations and Replies   120

Celebrations   131

Gifts and Thank-yous   147

Tipping   160

Index   181

Introduction

Some courtesies—never intentionally embarrassing another, never talking only about oneself, not gossiping, not prying, not asking personal questions, and not staring or pointing at someone, for example, are as old as time and, I fervently hope, will last in perpetuity.

Other courtesies have evolved as times have changed. Manners for using electronic communications and protocol for women executives dealing with male clients are examples of things our grandmothers never considered.

Good manners have always been based on common sense and thoughtfulness, and that hasn't changed. From the caution yet kindness required for interpersonal relationships to the graciousness that make celebrations special, there are times when our instincts tell us what to do. There are other times when we just aren't sure.

Part of the requirement for an increased focus on good manners is that there are more people in the world globally, and in our own towns and neighborhoods. Dealing with more people can make getting along with others more difficult than ever before. Whether we are apartment or backyard neighbors, practicing courtesies is increasingly important. The impact of a discourteous neighbor can be greater than it was in a less populated time because most of us tend to live closer together.

There are more of us in the workforce than ever before too, with a tendency toward less formality on the job. While this can be more comfortable, it also can be more confusing. It is not as easy to know how to address one another, or to be clear on the do's and don't's of socializing with and entertaining business associates.

Manners are sometimes based on safety. At-home good telephone manners of yesteryear have become unwise today. The chapter on communications updates what to say and how to say it, so you can better protect yourself and your family.

This book is arranged in such a way that it is easy to reference your question and find the most current solution to new-decade etiquette dilemmas. When times are so rushed, it is very nice to have ways to smooth the paths between people and establish the beginnings of pleasant relationships. Think of etiquette not as a strict set of rules, but as guidelines for our natural instinct for incorporating kindness and consideration into everything that we do. Manners are the tools that help us direct our desire to be thoughtful.

On these pages are more than 250 most-often asked questions about all kinds of situations that arise in all kinds of places, whether at home, in the neighborhood, at a restaurant, or at work.

There is a slogan I have seen lately on posters and T-shirts that augments the suggestions written on these pages: "Practice Random Acts of Kindness." Kindness and courtesy needn't always be deliberate and planned. Spontaneous kindness is an attribute of a person who already is well-mannered and courteous and whose natural instinct for courtesy is demonstrated in everything he or she does. When we get so busy and absorbed in what we have to do, it is nice to have a reminder that acts of kindness make our world a pleasanter place to live.

Relationships

Q. *My parents are divorced and unfriendly to one another. I am at a loss to know how to include everyone in special events such as my children's birthdays and holidays. How do I know which one to invite? When they both invite us for the same holiday, what do I do so that I don't hurt either one's feelings? They make me feel that I'm abandoning them. We also have my husband's parents to consider.*

A. Your sensitivity is admirable, but your priority is with your own family and the creation of holiday traditions that will become your children's own. You cannot make your parents' hostile relationship your problem. Be frank with each, telling them that you want special times to be relaxed and happy for your children. This means that you cannot spend Christmas, for example, driving to one's home and then the other's, and then to your husband's parents. Consider taking turns celebrating an event on its real date with one, and then have a second celebration on another day with the other.

Do not allow them to put you in the middle. Remind them that you love them both but insist that your children be able to spend time with *all* their grandparents in peace, happiness, and harmony.

Assuming that both your parents are otherwise lovely people, ask your in-law's if your mother or father could be invited to a holiday celebration at their house.

For those once-in-a-lifetime events that cannot be duplicated (a christening, graduation, recital, or wedding) ask your parents if, for the sake of their grandchildren, they couldn't "bury the hatchet" for that day so both could be present.

Q. *My ex-husband and I live in the same town. Our son lives with me, but his stepmother, who has children from a previous marriage, is involved in the same school activities. Her children use their father's last name while her last name is the same as my son's and mine. How do we avoid confusion?*
A. There is no way to avoid confusion except by explaining. Eventually, people will figure out who's who. When someone unfamiliar with your situation gets confused, simply say, "Timmy is my son. His father is now married to Sally Anderson. Her children are Janet and Jackie Smith."

Q. *I have been married for less than a year. My husband has a fourteen-year-old son from a previous marriage. I think we have established a good relationship. He has a mother who lives nearby. I'm not sure what my role is supposed to be with her. We do meet every so often. Do you have any advice?*

A. Good manners dictate that you are at least civil and polite, at most friendly. Good sense dictates that you don't discuss the state of your marriage. As for your stepson, don't give unsolicited advice, although you could offer help: "I know Jason has an orthodontist appointment on Friday. . . would it help if I drove him?" If your stepson lives with her most of the time, you can ask her advice about when he visits with you. Questions about his regular bedtime, a curfew she has established, medical care, or other things having to do with her house rules would reassure her that you respect her philosophy and are seeking to support it. Naturally, you would share any discussions of this nature with your husband.

Q. Whom do you tell about a divorce?
A. Tell those to whom it makes a difference. Tell your parents and close family and good friends. Tell your business associates only if they are good friends. Tell the landlord or superintendent and doorman if one of you is keeping the apartment. At times it is necessary to tell doctors and dentists if your children's bills are to be sent to the parent not in custody of the children, and it is wise to notify the school office and your children's teachers. It is important that they know of any situation that may have an impact on your children's behavior and school performance. Otherwise, it is not necessary to tell anyone. The situation will become public knowledge very quickly when one member of the couple moves out. The one who moves may have change-of-name and -address cards printed, and of

course his or her Christmas cards will serve as
announcements. A note may be added to them: "As
you can see, Bob and I are divorced. Hope to hear
from you at my new address."

Under no circumstances should printed divorce
announcements be sent out. It is in the worst of taste.

Q. *What name does a divorced woman use?*
A. A divorced woman does not continue to use her
husband's first name and is addressed as Mrs. Mar-
garet Thune, not Mrs. Andrew Thune.

Q. *Does a married woman's name differ from the
form a widow uses?*
A. No. A woman who is currently married and a
widow generally use the same form, "Mrs. George
Yost." A widow may use her first name if she wishes,
but then she may be mistaken for a divorcée. Many
older women prefer to continue using their husband's
name.

Q. *Besides one's parents who should be told about a
living-together relationship?*
A. Relatives need be informed of your new situation in
life only as they are involved with your life: siblings
whom you see or correspond with—yes; aunts, uncles,
and cousins with whom you are in close contact—yes;
but the "funeral and wedding relations"—no need.

Of course you tell the friends you see frequently
and those to whom you write often. In short, tell

anybody who will meet your partner on more than a casual basis and anyone with whom you regularly share the news of your life. You need not announce your relationship to business associates unless you see them socially, but if it comes up in conversation, do not hide it.

It is a good idea to tell the letter carrier that Victor Mangin or Susan Gleason will also be receiving mail at your address from now on. There is no need for further explanation.

Tell your landlord, the superintendent, and the door attendant if you have them, so that they will treat your new roommate as another tenant, not as a visitor.

Unless you know your neighbors well there is no need to say anything to them, other than a casual introduction if you meet. Nor is there any need to alert local shops. When your partner orders something to be delivered, the address given will be adequate.

Q. What do you call your living-together partner?
A. I have come to the conclusion that the best form of introduction is to use no word of definition at all. Merely say, "This is Natalie Desreyaud," or "I'd like you to meet Chet Nevins." It is simply not necessary to indicate the relationship between two people when you are at a gathering where relationships make little difference. In a small group where who relates to whom has more importance, all you need add to the introduction is "the man (or woman) I live with."

Q. *It has been a long time since I have been on a date. Now that I am single again, I need a refresher course on who pays for what, or whether I should just pay my own way, and on whether I can issue an invitation or must wait to be asked.*

A. Fortunately, dating etiquette has changed. Women don't have to sit by the phone hoping someone will call, and men don't have to carry the entire financial burden. When two people meet and sense that they would like to spend more time together, either may initiate a date. As to who pays, the guidelines are the same as they would be for two friends of the same gender. When an invitation is worded "would you have dinner with me on Saturday night?" the person inviting expects to pay, whether male or female. When two people decide, jointly, to buy tickets to an event or to meet for a meal, each would pay his or her own way, unless one insists on the other being his or her guest.

If a relationship develops and one feels that the other is paying most of the costs of their dates, he or she should initiate plans and firmly say, "this evening is my treat," or "I'd love to go, but I'll pick up the tickets this time."

Q. *When walking down the street are men expected to walk closest to the curb or to the buildings?*

A. The practice of men walking nearer the curb began as a way to protect women from runaway or obstreperous horses and splashing mud from carriage wheels on unpaved roads. Although the reason no longer exists, the pattern has been established and still is followed. If a man chooses to ignore the curbside rule, he should always walk on the woman's left.

Q. Does the "ladies first" rule always apply?
A. In most circumstances, indoors or out, a couple walks side-by-side. When necessary to walk single file the woman precedes the man, to follow a waiter to a table for instance. There are times, however, when a man goes first:

Over rough ground, he walks beside her and offers his hand if she needs assistance.

He steps ahead of her to open a car door for her to enter.

He gets out of a car first and holds the door for her when they arrive, unless she doesn't want to wait.

He precedes her down a steep or slippery stairway. However, he follows her up or down an escalator unless she asks him to go first to help her on or off.

He makes the gesture of stepping into a boat first, or off a bus first, to be ready to help her, unless she prefers that he not do so.

He steps into a revolving door that is not already moving ahead of a woman, but she precedes him through one that is already moving.

Q. Are men still expected to give up their seats for women on trains and buses? What about children giving up seats to adults?

A. A man is not expected to give up his seat unless a woman is elderly, infirm, pregnant, or burdened with a baby or a heavy armful of any sort. Otherwise it is to be assumed that a man who has worked all day is just as tired as the women on the train or bus. Of course a man may offer his seat to any woman if he wishes, and she may accept or refuse his offer as she wishes.

Children, on the other hand, should be taught to offer their seats to older people, both men and women. Generally, youngsters are strong, they have not usually worked as hard, and furthermore, it is a gesture of courtesy and respect.

Q. Who gets off the elevator first, men or women?
A. In a crowded elevator, whoever is nearest the door gets off first, whether men or women. In elevators that are not crowded or apartment or private elevators, a woman precedes a man out the door, just as she would in any room in a house.

Q. Should a couple walk hand in hand down a crowded street? Are there any acceptable public displays of affection?
A. There is nothing wrong with walking hand in hand in public, unless doing so causes pedestrian traffic to be impeded. In this case, single file is the rule until the sidewalk is less crowded. The only acceptable forms of public displays of affection are holding hands and

casual or affectionate kisses or hugs when greeting or saying goodbye. Other physical displays of affection should take place in private.

Q. Since my divorce I have begun dating a woman who seems interested in establishing a physical relationship and I am concerned about AIDS and other diseases. How do I discuss this without offending her?
A. It is very difficult and extremely embarrassing to most people to ask, "What have you been doing, with whom, and when?" My opinion is that if you are willing to bare all with someone else, you should also be able to bare your thoughts.

Some sexually transmitted diseases (STDs) have cures. Others do not. A moment of passion, no matter how blissful, is not worth the ending of your life, prematurely and painfully.

With someone you have only recently met, there is absolutely nothing wrong with saying, "I'm sorry, but until we know each other better and feel more comfortable talking about sex, we just can't get involved in a sexual relationship. There is too much at risk."

If she or he becomes insulted, so be it. You aren't after all, casting aspersions upon his or her character, but neither you nor he or she has any idea with whom each other's previous sexual partners have been intimate, and that is how disease is spread— from one person, to the next, to the next.

With someone with whom you are considering establishing a long-term relationship, you must talk openly. Never name names, but if you or he or she has had an active sex life, it is only fair to the other to have or to request a blood and medical checkup to make sure you are healthy and not carrying disease. This may seem offensive, but people have been known to lie about the results of such tests and it is not out of line for you to insist that you exchange results before entering into any intimate relationship.

And, as often as people eschew condoms, they are, while not a guarantee, a protection against disease. A woman has every right to insist that her partner wear one; a man has every right to wear one. It is not a sign of true love to throw precaution to the wind just to avoid insulting a sexual partner.

Q. My mother-in-law is full of advice and quick to blame me for anything that goes wrong. If my four-year-old gets an ear infection, it is my fault because she wasn't wearing a hat. My husband only likes her meat loaf and I should use her recipe (even though my husband told me her meat loaf was always so greasy he gets nauseous just thinking about it). How can I tell her, politely, of course, to keep her opinions to herself?
A. As you have probably discovered, there is no polite way to do this. Whatever you say will be viewed as criticism and do nothing to strengthen family relationships. The woman who raised your husband is having a difficult time not being the center of his life. You probably wish she had a higher opinion of you and certainly resent her implied criticisms. I don't blame you for any resentment you feel. But I

caution you that you can't win in a confrontation nor change her behavior and suggest that you, in essence, grin and bear it. Any conflict only puts your husband miserably in the middle, and I doubt you'd want him to sever his relationship with his mother, or your children's relationship with their grandmother. She is being ill-mannered, intrusive, and rude. You should be beautifully mannered, thank her for her advice, and change the subject.

Q. *What should a newlywed call his or her spouse's parents?*
A. There is no definite answer to this question. The choice of names is personal. The parents, simply because they are older, should take the initiative and suggest a name that their new daughter-in-law or son-in-law should call them if there is awkwardness or if he or she is still calling them "Mr. and Mrs." If the parents do not make the first move, it is perfectly all right to ask them what they'd like to be called, since "Mr. and Mrs." sounds too formal. One option you may consider is to call your in-laws "Mom and Dad B," using the initial of their surname if you aren't comfortable calling them "Mom and Dad." reserving that for your parents.

Q. *What names should children use when addressing their parents' friends?*
A. They should call them "Mr." or "Mrs." unless their parents' friends have requested that they call them by their first names or by nicknames.

Q. *My husband is named after his father and uses the suffix "Jr." after his name. We are naming our son after my husband's uncle. Do we attach a suffix after his name, and if so, would it also be "Jr."?*

A. Yes, he may receive a suffix after his name, but the suffix is "2nd." A child named after his grandfather (whose name is different from the child's father's), uncle, or cousin also is called "2nd," not "Jr." Were your son to be named after his father, who is named after his own father, the suffix would be "3rd."

Q. *Are there any guidelines for insisting on good manners from my children's friends? For example, my daughter's boyfriend wears his baseball hat at the table when he has dinner with us and we don't allow hats at the table. My son's friend snaps and cracks his gum when he is talking to us, which bothers me. What may I say to them?*

A. You have to draw the line between the "When in Rome" rules of etiquette and commentary on someone else's personal manners, or lack thereof. You have every right to say, "Brian, one of our house rules is 'no hats at the table,' so please park yours in the hall for now." This should be said in private, before he is actually seated at the table. You don't really have the right, however, to tell a child who is not your own that it is rude to chew gum loudly, or that he should wear deodorant, or that he should stand up when an adult enters the room, unless he has asked you for advice. You can only hope that the example set in your home inspires him to acquire similar manners and practice them in the future.

Getting Along with Others

Q. *When visiting the home of friends who own pets can I, without appearing rude, protest their dog's jumping on me or their cat's sitting on my lap?*
A. Yes. Remain pleasant and ask that the animal be put in another room. Say, "I'm sorry, but cats (or dogs) really bother me—" or "My allergies have gotten so much worse—would you mind removing Tabby (or Fido) from the room until I leave?"

A good host will automatically keep animals away when visitors are new acquaintances, to make sure his cat or dog doesn't bother the guest. Although the host is quite used to his pet's jumping into laps, etc., guests are not and they need not be subjected to animals who are not perfectly behaved.

Q. *What do you consider the hallmarks of being a good neighbor?*
A. Being a good neighbor is mainly a matter of applying the Golden Rule. Treat your neighbors as you would like them to treat you. Allow them their privacy, be tolerant, communicate problems or annoy-

ances directly with them, not with others, and remember that the fact that you live close to each other does not mean you or they should be included in all the other's activities. Even if good neighbors become good friends, you and they have other friends and neither of you should expect to be included every time one of you entertains.

Q. *Can you offer any guidelines for apartment living?*
A. The best guideline, as with many rules of etiquette, is the consideration of others. Don't do things you wouldn't want done to you. Don't deface property, litter, allow garbage to build up, or be insensitive about noise. Children's play may not seem loud, nor does the radio, stereo, or television set when you're in the same room with them, but those sounds carry easily from one apartment to another. Although some noise is to be expected, it is not to be expected at the crack of dawn or late at night. At these times, noisemaking should be eliminated. At others, if the decibel level is very high, with dogs barking, children screaming, or babies crying, sounds should be softened as much as possible by shutting the windows if necessary.

Q. *How should people behave in public places, like parks, playgrounds, and beaches?*
A. People should behave in public as they would in their own homes or yards, by cleaning up after themselves, not by behaving as though there was a hired staff to follow behind and restore to order what they destroy.

At the beach, there are additional considerations:

Avoid crowding. Don't choose a spot right next to someone already there.

If you have children in tow, choose a spot close to where they will play so they don't need to run past other people to get there and back, splashing water and kicking sand.

Loud radios and tape players are an intrusion on others. Wear earphones, or keep the volume so low only you can hear it.

Public displays of affection are distasteful and especially uncomfortable for people with children. Save physical contact for private.

Practice good taste in beach apparel. Unless you are specifically at a private beach, keep your swimming attire up, on, and fastened, and appropriate to your figure type and body weight.

Leave public grounds cleaner than you found them. If everyone cleaned up his own mess plus one item more, our countryside would soon regain the beauty it has in many places lost.

Q. *Whether my young daughter and I are at the beach or the park, there always is another child who wants her toys. How do I work out the difference for her between sharing and the right to her own possessions when she shouldn't have to share, as with a stranger?*

A. Helping children learn to share their toys gives

them useful skills for later in life. There is a limit, however. If a mother gets huffy because your daughter won't share her sand shovel with her son, a stranger who has admired it and wants it, you should ask whether she would hand over her car keys to you when you admire it and demand access to it. You can explain the difference to your daughter by saying that children share with those who are less fortunate, with friends and acquaintances, and in group situations. She would share when she invites a friend to her house, and she would expect a friend to share when invited to her house. She should not expect someone she has never seen before to offer her his toys, however, nor should she take someone's toys just because she wants them. In the same way, she has the right to *not* share with someone she doesn't know. The fact that a playground or beach is public does not mean that what we take to it becomes communal property.

Q. *The law has pretty much eliminated any questions about smoking in public places, but is it all right to smoke in a friend's home?*

A. It is safe to assume that you are not to smoke in anyone's home unless they do themselves. Today with unanswered questions about the dangers of secondhand smoke, even those who previously didn't mind may mind now. If you must have a cigarette, ask your host or hostess if you could step outside for a few minutes for one. Even when your host smokes cigarettes, you should not light a pipe or cigar indoors unless there are no other guests and he insists that he loves the smell. Never smoke around infants or small children.

When at a party in a club where smoking is allowed, it still is courteous to ask those with you if they mind if you smoke. Lastly, remember not to walk around or dance with a cigarette in your hand or mouth.

Q. *My neighbor's cat has made my garden her litter box. Is there an acceptable way to complain?*
A. When cats are given access to the outdoors it is hard to control where they go or what they do, so this is a difficult problem. The alternative would be for your neighbor to keep the cat indoors or for you to fence your garden in such a way that it is difficult for the cat to enter it. If the latter is not possible, then you can register a complaint, explaining that, as your neighbor may have noticed, you spend hours gardening, but that it has become unpleasant because his cat has taken it over. Ask if there is any way he could help keep his cat out of your garden. At least he will be aware that you mind, and perhaps will find his own solution.

Q. *My town does not have a law regarding picking up after a dog. Many dog-walkers do this anyway, but there is one person in my neighborhood who walks her dog past my house every day. Without fail, he stops and uses my front yard. I then have to scoop up what he has left behind. Should I say anything?*
A. Yes. The next time you see them coming, walk

out to greet them. Simply say that you enjoy seeing them walk by and understand that the dog needs to "go," but that since he frequently selects your yard as a rest stop, you find yourself cleaning up after him regularly. Say that you don't enjoy this, and ask that the neighbor please pick up after her dog. You can then ask a friendly question, such as the dog's name, or how old the dog is, chat a moment, and say farewell. If you find that this neighbor disregards your reasonable request, then you should continue to make it until she is so embarrassed that she takes a different route, or until she learns to clean up after her own dog.

Q. *My dog is very well behaved. Is there any reason that I can't take her with me when I visit friends?*
A. The best reason is that if the dog is not invited, she should stay at home. Unless you *know* that the person you are visiting loves animals, never just show up with a pet or ask whether you may bring a pet along on a visit. Your host and hostess may be great dog lovers, but they may not want a strange dog who may or may not get along with their dog. You are putting them in a difficult position if they are not enthusiastic about your request. If they make the suggestion, naturally your pet may go. Be sure, before you accept on his behalf, that his behavior will be exemplary. You should never, ever take a dog that is not perfectly house-trained, chews things, or will not stay off furniture to anyone else's house.

Q. How do you deal with ethnic slurs made in a social situation?
A. You should feel no need to laugh or support such a display of poor taste. You may quietly say, "I don't appreciate that kind of remark," or "I dislike jokes that put others down." If the offensive slurs continue, you may simply take your leave.

If there are people of the targeted group with you or in hearing range, your situation is more embarrassing. Try to change the conversation if you can. If you cannot, avoid the urge to rise to the defense, which might evoke an onslaught even more embarrassing to your friends. Keep your silence, break away when possible, and apologize profusely to them in private.

If you belong to the group under attack you have two choices. You can ignore it and avoid those people in the future. Or, you can say: "You must be talking about me. I'm Irish (or whatever it is)." Their shocked embarrassment can be almost as rewarding as their limp efforts to make amends and perhaps this will temper their prejudice in the future.

Q. How should I behave around physically disabled people?
A. Ideally, you behave just as you would around a person who has no visible disability. Never stare, and never race in to seize someone's arm or grab a wheelchair. If a disabled person appears to be having difficulty, ask if, and in what way, you can be of assistance. Never make personal remarks or ask personal ques-

tions. If the disabled person wishes to discuss his or her condition, he or she may introduce the subject— you may not. If he or she does bring it up, never, never pry into feelings or clinical symptoms—subjects that disabled people may be doing their best to forget.

Q. I am sometimes embarrassed about not knowing how to act when dealing with hearing-impaired or deaf people. Can you offer any hints?
A. There are many degrees of deafness, from partial loss of hearing in one ear to complete deafness. If you know that the hearing loss is in one ear, it is considerate to sit on the side of the good ear anywhere it isn't possible to sit face to face. In the case of total hearing loss, the only means of communication is visual, through lip-reading or sign language.

> When talking, speak slowly and distinctly. Don't use exaggerated lip movements that can be confusing to a person who has been taught to read normal lip movements.
>
> Don't shout to attract the person's attention. Either it does no good since he can't hear you anyway or it causes distortion since hearing aids are usually adjusted to the normal tone of voice.
>
> Be patient while talking and willing to repeat or rephrase.

If a relative or close friend is hearing-impaired, recommend that he or she get and wear a hearing aid. There is no more stigma attached to this than there is to wearing glasses. Encourage participation in family and social activities since persons with severe disabilities tend to withdraw into themselves. Try to be sensitive to their reactions, however, because too much pressure can have the opposite effect from that desired. Always include them in conversation, making sure they can see you or the group.

Q. *When I meet blind people I sometimes find myself speaking more loudly, probably because I don't really know what to do and am uncomfortable in their presence. How should I act?*

A. What you need to keep in mind is that in every other respect blind people are probably exactly like you. Blind people's other faculties are in no way impaired and may be more sensitively developed to compensate for their loss of sight.

When talking, use a normal voice.

Don't avoid the use of the word *see*. A blind person uses it as much as anyone else.

If you are in a room with a blind person it is courteous to describe the room setting and identify the others in the room.

It is correct to ask a blind person if you can help him or her cross the street, but never grasp his or her arm or try to give assistance without first asking whether you may. Let the blind person take your arm rather than your propelling him or her.

When walking with a blind person mention any

upcoming obstacles, a step for instance, or a corner to be turned.

If the blind person has a guide dog, do not attempt to play with or distract the dog in any way. Its attention must remain fully on its master, whose safety and well-being depends on the dog's strict adherence to its training.

Q. *How long should a visitor stay when calling on a sick friend, either at home or in the hospital?*
A. Plan to stay no more than fifteen or twenty minutes, and stick to it, no matter how much your friend may urge you to stay. If other visitors arrive while you are there, leave sooner so that they may have their share of the patient's time without overtiring him or her.

Q. *What can I do if children of friends are brought along on an adults-only visit?*
A. If you wish to be gracious you must invite them in. If the children are small, however, and you have valuable objects that could be damaged, you may ask them to wait a moment while you remove the objects from harm's way, mentioning that you weren't expecting the children. If you have paper and pencils on hand, you can put them out on your kitchen table for an activity, offer a snack, or find a suitable program on television to keep the children occupied while you and your friends talk.

Other than providing these diversions, you are

not obligated to entertain the children and it is the parents' responsibility to be sure they are well behaved and occupied.

Q. Several of my friends have young children. I do not. What preparations can you suggest making before they visit?
A. Remove from low tables breakable articles and things that might be dangerous to a small child. Shut the doors to rooms you wish to make "off limits," and make sure doors to cellar steps and low windows are tightly closed or locked. After completing your safety check, put together a basket of simple toys— coloring books, crayons, blocks, even plastic and wooden cooking utensils and pots and pans. These go a long way toward making the visit enjoyable for both parent and host. If you have absolutely nothing on hand to entertain a child, you may ask that the parents bring a bag of toys so the child or children can be kept busy and happy during the visit. It's also a good idea to have a supply of cookies or crackers and milk or juice on hand to fill in when the novelty of playing in a different environment wears off.

Q. Am I obligated to entertain an unexpected guest?
A. No, if you have prior plans, those plans take precedence over entertaining an unexpected guest. If someone arrives unexpectedly from quite a distance and you are planning to leave for a church supper or an informal buffet or cocktail party, check with your host and if all right, suggest your guest go along with

you. If, however, you are expected at a small dinner party or for bridge, ask your guest to make him- or herself at home until you return. You should, if possible, find something in the refrigerator or cupboard that will serve as a snack or light meal. You need not make yourself late for your appointment by taking the time to prepare a full meal, although you should show your guest where the ingredients are if he or she wishes to do so.

When the visitor is from nearby, you merely say frankly, "I'm terribly sorry, but we were just leaving for the theater. Could you come back another time?" But make the future date right then. "Another time" left at that means little, but a firm invitation proves that you would really enjoy a visit at a more convenient time. If your earlier plans were such that they could be carried out on another day, it would of course be more polite to postpone them and stay at home with your visitor.

If you are just about to start your dinner when friends drop in, you must try to make the meal stretch to include them. If they say, "Oh, no thank you—we've just eaten," pull up a chair for them, offer them a cup of coffee or a cold drink, and ask their forgiveness while you finish your meal.

Q. I try to volunteer as much as possible in my community. A few times, I have been teamed with others who do not do their own share of the work, leaving me to do it myself. Would it be rude to point this out?
A. Yes, because it would serve no purpose. Doing so

may even make it look like you are whining about how hard you worked, or as if you are seeking praise. If possible, be discriminating in the future about the persons with whom you share responsibilities. If one of those who dumped her work on you in the past indicates that she wants to work with you again, just say, "Oh, I'm sorry Molly, I'm already working with Janet! I know they need more help on the planning committee, though."

Q. Three friends and I were having tea when one of them turned to another and whispered something in her ear. I thought this was rude and felt offended. What is your opinion?
A. I agree with you. It is very rude to whisper in front of other people.

Q. Some of my neighbors are Jewish but speak often of Christmas as though they perhaps celebrate it some-what. When they wish me a very Merry Christmas would it be appropriate for me to say "and the same to you?"
A. Rather than responding this way, say, "And a happy Hanukkah to *you*." They are respecting your faith. You respect theirs in return when you acknowledge their special days and celebrations.

Q. A new friend of mine is Protestant. I am Jewish. I know little about his faith and am a little embarrassed about expressing my ignorance, plus, I don't want to offend him by asking him about something he may consider private. Would it be inappropriate to ask him to explain it to me?

A. Of course not. If he practices his faith it is important to him and you are being both polite and thoughtful in asking him to talk about something that is meaningful to his life. Surely, somewhere in life, you had a teacher say to you, "There is no such thing as a stupid question." This is particularly true between friends. While he may not feel comfortable sharing his innermost religious thoughts with a new friend, he could not be uncomfortable explaining the basic tenets of his religion.

Q. I would like to know the correct thing to do with bedding the next morning when staying overnight at a friend's.

A. Remove the sheets and pull up the bedspread neatly. Fold the sheets and leave them at the foot of the bed or take them to the laundry room. Your hostess can then make up the bed at her leisure.

Q. I always ask my company to take off their shoes because I don't want my new rugs and carpets soiled. Some oblige graciously; some oblige but get offended. What do you suggest?

A. If you can lay a piece of indoor-outdoor carpeting leading to your entry and a good doormat at the door, your carpets should not get soiled. If you still feel you must ask people to remove their shoes, buy a supply of slippers such as the airlines give out on long trips and put them by the door for guests to use.

Q. *What do you consider the hallmarks of a good guest? Of a good host and hostess?*
A. A good guest is enthusiastic, congenial, and considerate, treating other guests and the host and hostess, as well as their property, with thoughtfulness and respect. A good host and hostess are well prepared to see to the needs of each of their guests, having carefully planned for their comfort and entertainment.

Q. *The invitation says dinner at 7:30. What time should I arrive at the party?*
A. The answer depends on the custom in your area. If the custom is that guests are not expected to arrive until fifteen minutes to half an hour after the stated hour, it is wise to follow this practice. Otherwise you should arrive no later than 15 minutes after the hour given and never earlier.

Q. *When a party is given in someone's honor is he supposed to be the first guest to leave or the last?*
A. Traditionally he is supposed to be the first to leave but this rule is obsolete, so the guest of honor may feel free to stay as long as he likes. The only time this rule is followed is when the guest of honor is the President of the United States, in which case no one may leave before he does.

Q. *How long should a hostess delay dinner for a late-arriving guest?*
A. Fifteen minutes is the established length of time. To wait more than twenty minutes, at the outside,

would be showing rudeness to many for the sake of one. When the late guest finally arrives, he or she of course apologizes to the hostess and then is seated.

Q. *When a guest arrives late and we've already finished the first course, is that course served to the late-arriving guest?*

A. No, the latecomer is served whatever course is being eaten at the time he or she arrives, unless the course is dessert, in which case he or she would be served the entrée while others have their dessert.

Q. *How long should a guest remain at a party, or in other words, how do I know to call it a night?*

A. Try to be sensitive and aware of the people around you. Most hostesses are reluctant to try to "speed the parting guest" so make an effort to observe when your hosts—and others at the party—begin to look tired, and make the move to break it up yourself. You should remain for at least one hour after dinner, as it is hardly complimentary to the hostess to "eat and run." At a small party you should not leave long before anyone else seems ready to go, because your departure is very apt to break up the party.

Q. *How do you take your leave at a large party? A small gathering?*

A. At a large party, locate your host and hostess, wait until they are free to speak to you for a moment, and thank them for a lovely evening. Insist that there is no need for them to see you to the door, find your coat or ask the maid, if there is one, and let yourself out.

At a small gathering, say your goodbyes to the other guests, thank your host and hostess, find your coat, and leave. Nothing is more irritating than the guest who gets her coat, says goodbye to the other guests, and twenty minutes later is still standing in the open door talking with her hostess.

Q. *If everyone is having a good time would it be rude of the hosts to encourage their guests to remain longer?*
A. Not at all! It shows you are enjoying their company too, and if their offer to leave seems tentative, it is far friendlier to say, "Oh, don't go—it's Friday night and we can all sleep late tomorrow morning," than to jump up and bring them their coats the minute someone says, "Well, it's getting late . . . " If, however, they really must leave, one suggestion that they stay is enough. Don't force them to remain if they have a baby-sitter waiting or are firm in their resolve to go.

Q. *How can I discourage my guests from mixing their own drinks in my home?*
A. It is difficult to do without being insulting. You can control the situation somewhat, however, by going to the bar with your guest and asking them to get out the ice or the mix or whatever while you pour the liquor yourself. You can also avoid having more than one bottle of liquor in evidence if guests seem to be heavy drinkers, and you can make it obvious that you use a jigger to pour drinks and hand the jigger to your guests before they pour themselves.

Q. How do I handle an inebriated guest?

A. You must refuse to serve him or her more liquor. He or she may become insulted and abusive, but that is preferable to having him or her become more intoxicated. You are then responsible for seeing that a drunken guest is taken home. You may ask a good friend to drive him or her, or you can go yourself if the distance isn't great, or you can call a cab, give the directions, and pay for it. The person's car keys should be taken away if he or she is not willing to be taken home by someone else. If your guest has reached the point of almost passing out, two or three other guests should help him or her to a bed to sleep it off overnight. If the inebriated person has a spouse or date present, you should offer this person accommodations too, or see that he or she gets home safely.

Q. I got drunk at a party. Should I have called my hosts the next day and apologized?

A. Yes, if your behavior was insulting or rude and if you disrupted the party you should apologize immediately. If you felt yourself getting drunk, however, and left the party without embarrassing yourself, the other guests, or your hosts, there is really little to apologize for except perhaps an early departure. You can mention this when you make your thank-you call by saying, "Your party was terrific! I'm sorry to have left a little early, but I had too much to drink and thought it was best to go before I passed out on your couch."

Q. *May I offer to help my hostess serve or clear the table?*
A. Yes, you may offer, but don't insist if she refuses your help. Most hostesses want you to relax or prefer to follow their own system of organization by themselves.

Q. *I am the mother of a preschooler and an infant. My husband and I have several friends who come to visit and stay past 2 A.M.! Is it ever acceptable to ask them to leave. If so, how?*
A. Your friends must be childless or they would know better than to stay until 2 A.M. You may certainly suggest that they leave by saying, "Well, this has been great fun, but the baby will have us up by six or earlier and we've really got to get to bed. Let's get together again soon."

When guests outstay their welcome at a home where there are no children, it is also effective to say, with good humor, "Well, Pat, we'd better go to bed; these poor folks want to go home!"

Meeting and Greeting

Q. *What are the rules for making introductions? Are there forms that should be avoided?*
A. The overall rule is that one person is always introduced to another. This is achieved either by the actual use of the word *to*—"Mr. Benson, I'd like to introduce you to Mr. Smith"—or by saying the name of the person to whom the other is being introduced first, without using the preposition *to.* An example of this is: "Mrs. Newgaard, may I introduce Mr. Collier."

In addition to the overall rule, there are three basic rules:

1) A man is always introduced *to* a woman. "Mrs. Pullman, I'd like you to meet Mr. Havlin." "Janny, this is my cousin, John Vaccaro." "Mr. DeRuvo, may I introduce you *to* my mother, Mrs. Smithson."

2) A young person is always introduced to an older person.

    "Dr. Josephson, I'd like you to meet my daughter, Lily Peterson."

"Aunt Ruth, this is my roommate, Elizabeth Feeney."

3) A less important person is always introduced *to* a more important person. This rule can be complicated, since it may be difficult to determine who is more important. There is one guideline which may help in some circumstances: Members of your family, even though they may be more prominent, are introduced *to* the other person as a matter of courtesy.

"Mr. Connor, I'd like you to meet my stepfather, Governor Bradley."

"Mrs. Anselmi, this is my aunt, Professor Johnston."

The easiest way not to slip up is to always say the name of the woman, the older person, or the more prominent person first, followed by the phrase, "I'd like you to meet . . . " or "this is . . . " or "may I introduce . . . ." If you inadvertently say the wrong name first, correct your slip by saying, "Mr. Heath, I'd like to introduce you to Mrs. McGregor."

Yes, there are forms to be avoided:

Don't introduce people by their first names only. Always include a person's full name.

When phrasing your introduction, avoid expressing it as a command, such as "Mr. Bonner, shake hands with Mr. Heath," or "Mrs. Digby, meet my cousin, Barbara."

Avoid calling only one person "my friend" in an introduction. It implies that the other person isn't your friend.

When you introduce yourself, don't begin by saying, "What's your name?" Start by giving your own name: "Hello, I'm Joan Hamburg. . . "

Do not repeat "Mr. Jones . . . Mr. Smith. Mr. Smith . . . Mr. Jones." To say each name once is enough.

Do not refer to your spouse as "Mr. Jansen" or "Mrs. J." in conversation. Rather, refer to him or her as "my husband" or "my wife" in situations where first names are not being used.

Q. Are there occasions when first names aren't used? What are they?
A. Yes, there are. When meeting one of the following people first names may not be used except when they request it:

- A superior in one's business

- A business client or customer

- A person of higher rank (a diplomat, a public official, a professor, for example)

- Professional people offering you their services (doctors, lawyers, etc.). In turn, they should not use your first name unless you request them to.

- An older person

Q. Is it necessary to specify my relationship to some-one when introducing family members?
A. No, it is not necessary, but it is helpful to include an identifying phrase. This provides a conversational opening for strangers. Since you courteously give precedence to the other person when introducing a family member, the identifying phrase comes at the end of the introduction: "Mrs. Cottrell, I'd like you to meet my daughter, Deborah."

Q. How do you introduce your live-in partner?
A. Although you usually identify family members as such, you needn't identify boyfriends, girlfriends, or live-in companions with their relationship to you. Saying his or her name is sufficient.

Q. Should children introduce their parents by using first names?
A. It depends upon to whom they are making the introduction. One should always use the name that the newly introduced pair will use in talking to each other. If you are introducing your roommate to your father, he would, of course, call your father by the title "Mr." If you are introducing your roommate's father to your father, you would use your father's full name: "Mr. Davies, may I introduce my father, Franklin Palmer."

Q. How should stepparents be introduced?
A. There is nothing derogatory or objectionable in the terms *stepmother* or *stepfather,* and the simplest

form of introduction, said in the warmest tone to indicate an affectionate relationship, is: "Mrs. Hibbing, I'd like you to meet my stepfather, Mr. Brown." Even if you call your stepfather by his first name, he should be introduced to your peers or younger persons as "Mr. Brown," not "Jack."

Q. How should ex-family members be introduced?
A. If the introduction is very casual and it is not likely that any of the people involved will see each other again, no explanation is necessary. If the new acquaintanceship is likely to continue, it is important to explain the relationship as clearly as possible. A former mother-in-law would say, "I'd like you to meet Mary Dunbar. Mary is John's (or my son's) widow and is now married to Joe Dunbar." Had Mary been divorced, the mother-in-law would say, "Mary was John's wife and is now married to . . . " Mary's introduction of her former mother-in-law will be, "This is Mrs. Judson, Sarah's grandmother," or "my first husband's mother."

Q. How are professional women addressed in social situations?
A. A woman who is a medical doctor, a dentist, etc., is addressed by, and introduced with, her title, socially as well as professionally.

Q. I often forget people's names and am at a loss to introduce them to others. How can I make introductions under these situations?

A. There is nothing you can do but introduce the friend who has joined you to the person whose name you've forgotten by saying to the latter, "Oh, do you know Janet McCall?" Hopefully the nameless person will be tactful and understanding enough to announce his own name. If he doesn't, and your friend makes matters worse by saying, "You didn't tell me *his* name," it's even more embarrassing. The only solution is to be completely frank, admit you're having a mental block, and ask them to complete the introduction themselves.

Remember the feeling, however, and when you meet someone who obviously doesn't remember your name, or might not remember it, offer it at once. Say immediately, "Hello, I'm Julie Hopewell. I met you at the Anderson's last Christmas." Never say, "You don't remember me, do you?" which embarrasses the other person.

Q. What can I say when introduced besides "how do you do?"
A. Whether you say "how do you do" or "hello" when introduced to another, follow with the person's name, which helps commit the name to memory. Your tone of voice indicates degrees of warmth, and if you are introduced to someone you have wanted to meet, you can follow "How do you do, Mr. Struthers" or "Hello, Mrs. Jenson" with "I'm so glad to meet you—Jerry Ernst speaks of you all the time!" or whatever may be the reason for your special interest. If you are introduced and left standing with the

person you've just met, of course you would attempt further conversation. A positive comment on the occasion, the food, or even the weather are all safe and noncontroversial openers.

Q. I am often at a loss about starting a conversation with a stranger. Can you give me any hints to get the conversation going?
A. Don't ask questions that can be answered "yes" or "no." Instead, ask his advice or opinion. From his answer, hopefully you can carry on a conversation. Don't be afraid of a period of silence and try to fill it by chattering about anything at all.. Think before you speak. Dorothy Sarnoff wrote: "*I* is the smallest letter in the alphabet. Don't make it the largest word in your vocabulary. Say, with Socrates, not 'I think,' but 'what do you think?'" You will leave the person with the impression that you are an interesting and interested person. Just as important, you'll be remembered as a good listener when you don't monopolize the conversation. Of course, take your turn, describing something you have been doing or an interesting article you have read, but then stop and ask your new acquaintance his opinion about or experiences with the topic.

Q. How do you handle a tactless person who makes his prejudices known in social situations?
A. If you find another's opinion totally unacceptable, try to change the subject as soon as possible. If that doesn't work, excuse yourself from the conversation, particularly if you care intensely about the subject

and might become emotional in your response.

Q. *How do you answer personal questions about your age or the cost of a gift?*
A. If you are asked your age and would prefer not to give it, you might say, "Old enough to know better," or you can be as indefinite as, "Over twenty-one," or you can use my particular favorite, "Thirty-nine (or forty-nine, or whatever) and holding."

When you are asked the cost of a gift or your house or a piece of clothing, you are under no obligation to answer with the price. You can simply say, "I don't know (or remember) what it cost," or you can say, "I'd rather not talk about that, if you don't mind. With the cost of living what it is, the whole subject is too depressing . . ." and change the subject.

Q. *How do I correct my host or hostess when I've been incorrectly introduced?*
A. It is only sensible and kind to correct the error immediately, but not with annoyance. If possible, make light of it so as not to embarrass the host or hostess. All you need say is, "Actually, it's Tracey, not Stacey—people get it confused all the time! "

Q. *My name is a little unusual and frequently mispronounced. My new next-door neighbor has said it incorrectly for several months, to the point that it would really embarrass her if I corrected her now. What should I do?*
A. Explain the situation to a mutual friend and ask

her to correct your neighbor when it is a suitable time to do so. She can say, "You know, he pronounces his name Non, not Nan. It rhymes with John." Your neighbor may apologize or even ask you if this is true. If she does, naturally tell her not to think anything of it.

Q. *I never know whether or not to shake hands. Are there any guidelines to help me judge this situation?*
A. Yes, there are guidelines, but they are flexible and if someone is not aware of them, the guidelines should be overlooked and the proper response made.

For example, strictly speaking, it is a woman's place to offer her hand or not to a man, but if he should extend his hand first, she must give him hers. Technically, it is the place of a man to whom another is being introduced to offer his hand first, but the gesture is usually simultaneous.

Adults offer their hands to children first. If you think about it, the guidelines for shaking hands follow the guidelines for introductions: A woman offers her hand first; an older person initiates a handshake with a younger one; and the more important person, or the one to whom someone is being introduced, is the first to offer his or her hand.

Q. *Under what circumstances does a man rise when introduced to a woman? Do women stand when being introduced? Does it matter if the situation is social or for business?*
A. A man should rise when a woman comes into a

room for the first time and remain standing until she is seated or leaves the vicinity, or unless she says, "Thank you, but please sit down, I'm leaving in just a moment," or words to that effect. He does not jump up and down every time a hostess or another guest goes in and out.

When a client, whether woman or man, goes to a man's office on business, he should stand up and receive him or her, offer a chair, and not sit down until after the client is seated. When the client rises to leave he stands, escorts the client to the door, and holds the door for him or her. Neither a man nor a woman rises for a secretary or co-worker in the office.

A woman receiving a male client in her office may remain seated, but generally follows the same guidelines as given above for a man receiving clients in his office. Although she might remain seated if the client were a much younger person, she would definitely rise for a much older woman.

In a restaurant, when a woman greets a man in passing, he merely makes the gesture of rising slightly from his chair and nodding. If she pauses to speak for a moment, he rises fully and introduces her to others at his table.

Both the host and hostess always rise to greet each arriving guest. Members of the host's family, including young people, also rise as a guest enters the room, with the exception of a child who is sitting and chatting with an adult. He or she may continue the conversation, seated, unless the guest is brought over to be introduced, in which case the child should stand up instantly.

A woman does not stand when being introduced to someone at a distance, nor need she rise when shaking hands with anyone, unless the person is much older, very prominent, or is someone with whom she wants to go on talking. A woman should not jump to her feet for a woman who is only a few years older than she, since rising indicates, among other things, respect for age. The gesture, although well meant, would more than likely not be well received.

Communications

Q. Is it proper to send notes via the fax to friends?
A. Unless someone has a facsimile machine in his or her home which makes it a more private means of communication, the equipment is usually located at a central point in an office. Transmittals can be read by anyone who happens to be walking by the machine. A fax may be marked "confidential" but there is nothing confidential about the process. When the machine is located in an office, there is a cost factor that is paid by the company. For these two reasons, communications sent by fax should not be private, and unless it is a message that requires a moment of someone's time at work, it should not be sent to a place of business when its content is personal.

Q. What form should an E-mail letter follow?
A. As carefully as is possible, E-mail transmittals should follow the style of typewritten memos and be succinct and professional. While this kind of communication can be sent directly to someone's computer, it is not necessarily confidential or private so should

not be used for frivolous correspondence or messages of a personal nature.

Q. My penmanship isn't very good. May I type my personal letters?
A. Yes, it is absolutely correct to type a personal letter if writing is difficult. As more and more of us have computers and printers capable of producing lovely script your personal correspondence needn't look like a business letter anymore.

Q. How do you address correspondence to a married couple who use different surnames? Would the form of address differ if they were not married?
A. Correspondence to a married couple with different names should be addressed so that both names appear on the same line:

Mr. Jonathan Adams and Ms. Angela Blake

If the couple is unmarried, the names should be on separate lines:

Ms. Susan Amber
Mr. Howard Cole

Q. How should a married woman sign letters, with her business name or married name? Does it matter if the letter is for business or social purposes?
A. If a woman continues to use her own name in

business after marriage, she would sign business correspondence with her maiden name. If she uses her husband's name socially her personal correspondence would be signed with her first name and married name. If a woman uses her own name in business and socially all correspondence would be signed with her own name.

Q. *How is an envelope addressed to a couple when the woman uses her maiden name as part of her name?*
A. Most women do keep their maiden name as a middle name, but it is not ordinarily used when you are addressing an envelope to her and her husband, as a couple. She uses it in her signature—"Mary Field Smith"—and she may use it professionally. Letters to the couple are simply addressed to "Mr. and Mrs. John Smith." If she is hyphenating the two names, however, then the mail must be addressed to "Ms. Mary Field-Smith and Mr. John Smith."

Q. *What is the proper salutation at the beginning of a letter when you do not know the name and/or sex of the person to whom you are writing?*
A. "Dear Sir or Madam" is the best solution when you are writing to a person whose name and/or sex you do not know.

Q. *How is a letter addressed to a couple when the woman is a Dr. and her husband is a Mr.?*
A. You would write to "Dr. Lynn and Mr. Marc

Josephson." If she kept her maiden name professionally, you would write to "Dr. Lynn Finnigan and Mr. Mark Josephson."

Q. We have friends who are both dentists. How do we address their cards?
A. Letters to them should be addressed "Dr. Cynthia and Dr. James Haven" or to "Drs. Cynthia and James Haven."

Q. We have a woman pastor at our church. What is the proper way to address mail to her and her husband?
A. The proper form is "The Reverend Joan and Mr. John Smith."

Q. My husband is a psychologist and he worked hard to earn the title, Dr. However, I believe it is not proper for him to sign his name Dr. Doe when he signs the restaurant bill or another credit card slip. Am I correct?
A. Your husband should not sign his name "Dr. John Doe" just as another man does not sign "Mr. William Smith." He should be *addressed* as Dr., but his signature is simply "John Doe." To register in a hotel he signs "John Doe" unless you accompany him in which case he would sign "Dr. and Mrs. John Doe."

Q. What is the best way to address a letter to a male child. Is it Master to a certain age and then Mr.?
A. Traditionally, children were addressed as "Master"

until they were about six years old. Today "Master" is rarely seen. No title is used until boys graduate from college, at which time they became "Mr."

Q. *May I include my children's names on our Christmas card even though they both have their own apartments? I know they won't be sending cards to some of our old family friends and thought this was a way to extend a greeting from them.*

A. Ordinarily you do not sign for people not living under your roof. An alternative would be to sign your name and your husband's, and add a note that your children asked to be remembered to the receiver.

Q. *How do you feel about people sending Christmas cards detailing deaths of family members, illnesses, job losses, financial disasters, etc.? Three Christmases have been shadowed for me by cards from a college friend describing her progress with cancer. Surely a letter concerning these matters, if urgent, could be sent in November or January?*

A. I agree 100 percent. Christmas cards should be messages of faith, hope, and joy. They should not be used to purvey all of the terrible news that one must impart. That should be done in a separate message, preferably sent after Christmas when the sad tidings will not destroy the joy of the Christmas season.

Q. *Is it proper to send printed Christmas cards to family and friends? I have read that if you don't want to bother to sign your name, it is better to send no card at all. What do you think?*

A. Printed Christmas cards are perfectly acceptable as long as you add a personal note on those sent to friends and family. When they are sent to business associates it is not necessary to add to the printed signature.

Q. *Sometimes there are occasions when I send greeting cards to immediate neighbors. Often, I place them in a door newspaper box or the mailbox, but I wonder if they should be mailed instead?*

A. There is nothing wrong with slipping a card under a neighbor's door or placing it in the newspaper box. However, it is against U.S. Postal Service regulations to place unstamped mail in a mailbox so don't deliver your cards that way.

Q. *Over the years I have received several chain letters. Each one says that if I don't answer, I will disappoint everyone, or have something terrible happen to me. The letters are usually from very good friends. I not only mind complying, but I must also inconvenience six or more of my friends to continue the letter. What may I tactfully tell my friends when they ask why I haven't answered the letters?*

A. You are not alone in resenting chain letters. Most people find them a real imposition. They invariably try to make you feel guilty if you break the chain and usually they fall far short of their promise. The best way to handle it is to return the letter to the sender with a short note: "Sorry, just don't have time...etc."

and he can then send it to someone else to keep his chain going.

Q. *My family has chosen to shorten our very long surname to a more manageable one. How can we let everyone know we've done this?*
A. The quickest and simplest way is to send out formal announcements:

> Mr. and Mrs. Brian Malinowsky
> Announce that by Permission of the Court
> They and Their Children
> Have Taken the Family Name of
> Malin

Q. *What is the proper way to answer the telephone?*
A. The best way to answer the telephone at home is still "Hello." There is no need to identify yourself when answering your home telephone.

Q. *Does a caller give his or her name as soon as the phone is answered?*
A. Yes. Not only is it courteous, but it is helpful as well since it gives the person being called the chance to gather papers or whatever may be required by the caller, or to get to a more convenient telephone.

> To a maid you say: "This is Mrs. Franklin. Is Mrs. Henry in?"
> To a child you say: "This is Mrs. Franklin. Is your mother in?"

When you recognize the voice, say: "Hello, John. This is Helen. Is Sue there?"

When the person you are calling answers, say: "Hi, Sue. This is Helen," or "Hello, Mrs. Brooks. This is Helen Franklin."

An older person calling a younger one says: "This is Mrs. Franklin."

A young person calling an older man or woman says: "Hello, Mrs. Knox. This is Janet Frost."

A young child calling a friend says: "Hello, Mrs. Knox. This is Janet Frost. May I please speak to Tammy?"

If a caller does not identify him- or herself, it is correct to ask who is calling, even though it seems a little rude. Actually, the rudeness is on the part of the caller. It is also a matter of safety to inquire as to the identity of the caller. Many calls are made just to find out whether a house is empty, or whether there is an adult at home. If a woman or a child answering doesn't recognize the voice of the caller, he or she must say, "Who is calling, please?" If the name is unfamiliar and the caller does not further identify him- or herself, the answer must not be, "He's not home now." Instead say, "He's busy just now," or "He's not available just now—may he return your call?"

Q. *How do you respond to an invitation made by phone? Must you give an immediate response?*
A. It is incumbent on the person calling to explain the

invitation right away: "Hi, Joan, this is Kathleen. We're having a few people in Saturday night for dinner and bridge. Can you and Mark come?" It is most inconsiderate to ask "What are you doing Saturday night?" or "Are you busy Sunday afternoon?" without explaining why you want to know. A "we're not busy" answer could commit one to an evening of opera when one hates opera, and a "we're busy" answer, only to find out the invitation was for something terrific, is disappointing.

Therefore, if the caller does not have the courtesy to explain the invitation but asks only, "Are you busy Saturday night?" you may say, "I don't know if John has made any commitments for Saturday—I'll check with him. Why do you ask?" This forces the caller to issue a proper invitation.

Otherwise, it is very rude to say, "I'll let you know," unless it is immediately followed by an explanation, such as checking with a spouse for previous commitments or "we have tickets for the community theater group that night but perhaps I can exchange them for two on Friday—I'll call you back." Without this definite sort of reason, "I'll let you know" sounds as though you are waiting for a better invitation to come along.

Q. *How do you handle a wrong number?*
A. When you dial a wrong number, don't ask, "What number is this?" Ask instead, "Is this 555-0451?" so that you can look the number up again or dial more carefully the next time.

When you receive a wrong number call, don't give out your number to the caller. Simply inform him or her politely that the wrong number has been dialed.

Q. How should obscene calls be handled?
A. Hang up immediately. Don't give the caller the satisfaction of hearing you become upset or even responding. If, as sometimes happens, the call is repeated as soon as you hang up, leave the receiver off the hook for a little while.

If you are subjected to such calls regularly, notify the telephone company. They can try to trace the calls. If you have a callback service on your phone, or a device that shows the number of the person calling, you can report this to the telephone company who can then track the offensive caller even faster.

There is another effective remedy that will discourage the occasional caller. Keep an ordinary police whistle by the phone and as soon as you hear the first obscene word, blow a hard blast right into the telephone speaker. That caller will drop you from his list of victims there and then.

Q. Are business telephone manners different from social telephone manners?
A. Yes, business telephone manners differ from at-home telephone manners in several ways. When answering a business call, an assistant or secretary gives his or her supervisor's name: "Miss Moore's office (or Roz Moore's office). May I help you?" If people answer their phones directly, they usually

identify themselves: "Hello, this is Roz Moore" or simply, "Roz Moore."

The caller identifies him- or herself in this case, as with a personal or social call: "Hello. This is Tom Price. Is Miss Moore in?" or "Hello, Miss Moore. This is Tom Price. I'm with the Brownstone Company.

As with an at-home call, it is correct to ask the caller: "May I ask who is calling, please," if he or she fails to identify him- or herself. In an office, a secretary or assistant may also ask, "May I ask what this call is in reference to?" or less bluntly, "Will Miss Moore know what this call is about?"

Although it is not courteous to tie up a telephone line for long at home, it is particularly to be avoided in the office. Long personal conversations are not only out of place, but also wasteful of the time that belongs to the company, not to the employee.

Q. When I visit a friend and she answers the telephone and goes on to chat with the caller for ten or fifteen minutes I am offended. If it is a long distance call I can understand it, but when it is a local call I really think she could explain that she is busy and ask if she can call back. Am I wrong?

A. No, you are not wrong. You are quite right. No one should carry on an extended phone call when he or she has a visitor.

Q. I'm getting quite tired of calling someone and then being put on hold while she takes another call. Is there some guideline for using call waiting?

A. The only way to handle call waiting with any kind

of manners is to excuse yourself for a moment from your first call, answer the second call, take the number, and return immediately to the original call. When you are waiting for a call, or when members of your household are out and you think they may be calling for a ride or for help, you should say, at the beginning of a call, "Joan, I am expecting another call so you will have to excuse me if I respond to my call waiting if it rings." If Joan minds this, she can always call back later, or ask you to call when it is more convenient.

Q. One of the telephone services I have enables me to forward my calls to another number. Sometimes it is important for me to do this; when my children are out, for example, and might need assistance, or when I am waiting for an overseas call that is late and I have to go on to another appointment. Is it an intrusion on someone else to forward my calls to their number?
A. The best way to handle this is to call the person to whose number you would like to forward your calls and ask if it is all right. Explain why, and mention that there may be a few extraneous calls that come along with the one you are waiting for that will be a bother to her until you can get home again to disable the call forwarding function. If she doesn't mind, then it is a good idea to give her the gist of your message or questions in case the call comes between the time you put your telephone on forwarding and travel to her house or office.

On the Job

Q. *How important are manners at work? Isn't how well you do the job what is really important?*
A. Good manners are part of a job well done. Even when you work alone, there is often contact with others, whether it is an express delivery person, the night custodian, or a sales clerk at a store. Simple courtesy, which is what manners is all about, makes everyday interactions satisfactory. More than one executive has missed the opportunity for promotion by chewing with an open mouth at lunch, not rising to greet a visitor, or even because of a weak handshake and failing to make eye contact. Every member of a company should act as an ambassador of the organization. Bad manners are bad for business.

Q. *I do a lot of local traveling with my boss. We use the company car and driver. Am I supposed to sit in the front or the back?*
A. That's a good question. I actually know of a young executive who lost his chance for promotion because he sat in the roomier front seat, necessitating that the CEO climb into the back, already crowded by two

other members of the firm. Use common sense. When traveling by taxi, the least preferred seat is next to the driver. Take that seat if you are traveling with those senior to you. If it is the company limousine and several are traveling together, it may be that the best seat is in the front, allowing more leg and elbow room. If you aren't sure, don't be the first to rush to the car. Wait until your boss has chosen where he will sit, and then sit wherever there is room.

Q. *When starting a new job how do I know if I should use first names or address people by title and last name?*
A. At the beginning, it is safest to use "Mr.," "Mrs.," "Miss," or "Ms." If they say, "Please call me Mary (or Jim)," then you may feel free to do so. In return you should suggest that they call you by your first name as well.

Q. *I will soon be attending executive meetings as a junior person in my firm. How do I know where to sit if there are no name plates?*
A. You should wait to be told by a senior person where to sit. To avoid the appearance of hovering over the table, however, if no one gives you a direction, ask. Say, "Where would you like me to sit, Mr. Cassin?" It may be that it doesn't matter. But if it does, and you accidentally take a senior partner's seat, you are setting yourself up for the embarrassment of being asked to move.

Q. When my husband and I attend social functions for his company, he will kiss some of the female employees as well as his secretary as a "hello" Although this is a simple kiss on the cheek, I don't feel it is appropriate. Do you?

A. Kissing has no place in business surroundings among people who barely know each other or people who see each other all the time. A kiss is not a casual greeting but is an indication of real affection. If your husband had been away for a time and was greeting his employees after an absence, he might be justified in giving them a kiss in a social situation, but when he is working with them regularly, there is no justification for that type of greeting—even socially.

Q. There is a great deal of socializing in my company, in the form of weekend outings, dinner parties, and the like. Frankly, the hours I put in during the week are quite enough for me. I have a life outside of my office and resent the pressure to extend my weekdays through round-the-clock and weekend gatherings. I don't want to hurt my chances for promotion, but enough is enough! What should I do?

A. At all cost, you should hang on to your priorities. It is not uncommon for business to occupy much, if not most, of our leisure time. Your home life, family, and outside interests should certainly be at least as important as your career. It is also important to have friends and community involvement outside of your job, interests that remain should you lose your job or retire. For many years there was no question that business socializing was part of the path to success. Today an employee may feel pressured to narrow his or her life to the job and coworkers. Dedication to one's responsibilities, being able to say, every day, "that was a job well done," and devoting occasional or even frequent extra hours toward that job should be the criteria for promotion. Spending evenings and weekends demonstrating one's sociability and vying for executive attention should not.

Q. Occasionally some of my company's clients call me "dear." Often the comment comes from older clients, and perhaps they don't realize they are offending anyone, so I am hesitant to say anything. How can I politely encourage these clients to call me by my given name?
A. It is appropriate for you to say, "My name is Mary, not 'dear,' and I really prefer to be called Mary, please." Be sure, however, that you say it kindly and with the best of manners since, as you note, it is usually not intended as an offense.

Q. Does the salutation for a business letter differ from that on a personal letter?
A. No, there is no difference except that in a business letter the salutation is followed by a colon, while in a personal letter it is usually followed by a comma. What follows the word "dear" depends on your relationship with the recipient. If, when you speak to the vicepresident of marketing, you call him "Jim," you

would begin your letter with "Dear Jim." If you call him "Mr. Wallace" in person, your letter would begin "Dear Mr. Wallace."

Q. *How does a married woman sign business correspondence?*
A. She signs her first name and the last name she uses for business. Women and men alike do not use a title in their signature.

Q. *What is the proper way to use business cards? Are they ever used for social occasions?*
A. Business cards are never used for social purposes in the United States. They are limited to the use specified by their name: business. They are used in two main ways:

> When a business visit is made, a card is left as a record of the visit so that one's name, business firm, phone, and fax numbers are readily available. It is not necessary to leave a card on subsequent visits to the same firm.

> When executives meet people with whom they want to establish or further a business contact they give them their card. This could take place anywhere, from a convention to a cocktail party.

Q. *I can't tell you how many times I have picked up the phone to hear someone's secretary say: "Ms. Moore? Please hold for Mr. Jaffe." And I hold, and I* *hold, and I hold. These people are calling me. Why should I have to waste my time then waiting for them? Am I wrong?*

A. You are quite correct. It is inconsiderate and therefore rude for anyone to call you, engage your attention, and then keep you waiting. When a secretary places calls, his or her boss should be ready to pick up the phone as soon as contact is made.

Q. *May I invite my boss to lunch?*
A. No, never. You may return an invitation to his or her home, because that becomes a social occasion, but you never return a business lunch or dinner invitation. You do thank your boss, of course, anytime he or she has taken you to a business lunch or dinner.

Q. *When a group of business associates gathers for lunch, who pays?*
A. The one who issues the invitation is considered the host and it is expected that he or she pay for the lunch. If, on the other hand, a group of business associates plans to have lunch so they can spend an out-of-the-office hour together, each generally pays for his or her own lunch.

Q. *How does a businessman or -woman know if a social invitation includes spouses or partners?*
A. Usually the invitation is issued or addressed to both members of a couple. If, for some reason, you aren't sure if spouses are included, ask. If you are single, you should ask "shall I bring a date (or friend) or

would you rather I came alone?" If you are living with someone, your companion should be treated exactly as a spouse would be. If your partner has been excluded from the invitation because of your host's ignorance of the situation, all you need do is ask, "May I bring Susan Swanson, the woman I live with?" or "I live with Dave Ferris. Is it all right if I bring him?"

Q. *Whom from my work world should I invite to my daughter's wedding?*
A. If you are thinking of using your daughter's wedding to entertain clients, prospective clients, and business associates (and I hope you are not), be careful not to slight anyone by failure to extend an invitation. Also be careful not to diminish your daughter's day by inviting a lot of people she does not know or does not care to know. If the wedding is small and personal you should invite only those business people whom you consider personal friends.

Q. *Whom should I invite to my son's bar mitzvah?*
A. The answer depends on the size of the celebration of the occasion, as it does with a wedding. If the bar mitzvah is small and intimate, you need invite only friends, some of whom may be business associates. If it is large, you may want to invite the entire office. If the religious ceremony is not followed immediately by the party you may even decide to omit business invitations to the religious service, extending them only to the party afterward.

Q. What role does the spouse play in business entertaining?

A. A spouse's role is to support you—to make your guests feel welcome, to help them enjoy being with you both, as well as to assist with refreshments. It is also your spouse's role to listen well, to ask questions and to indicate the involvement of both of you in the company. Your spouse should feel free to discuss his or her profession and personal concerns, too, so long as the topic does not center on children and he or she does not monopolize the conversation.

Q. My husband and I are returning the dinner invitation of his employer by giving a small dinner party in our home. How does my husband extend the invitation?

A. The invitation should not be extended in person by your husband. Instead, you should write the invitation to your husband's boss and his or her spouse and mail it to their home.

Q. When giving a business dinner party at home without serving help must both my husband and I greet guests at the door?

A. Yes, whenever possible you both should be close by so introductions can be made. One of you can take the guests' wraps while the other takes them around the room and introduces them to people they do not know.

Q. My department head has asked four or five staff members and their spouses to dinner at his home. Do we treat this as an ordinary dinner invitation and take a gift of flowers or wine or candy? Should we purchase a gift as a group, or take separate gifts as individuals or couples?

A. If, in your community, you ordinarily take a small gift when you go to dinner, you should do the same in this instance. Since the gift is simply a token of thanks for hospitality, it doesn't seem necessary to purchase a group gift. However, if there is something you think your department head would enjoy that has a value greater than one would spend on a host/hostess gift individually and wish to contribute to it as a group. I see nothing wrong with this, with one exception: When the invitation is just to a few members of the department, your talking about the fact that you were invited may cause those who weren't invited to feel left out. This situation could make your boss feel uncomfortable.

Q. A friend who has just become an insurance agent has asked to review our various policies to see if she can do better for us. I've always felt it is wiser not to mix friendship and business—what do you think?

A. In general, I would agree with you. When one has a wide range of friends in a variety of service businesses, however, giving them your business is often an extension of that friendship—with one caveat: If something goes wrong; if the new muffler on your car falls off; if your case in court is not successful; if your investment is slower to show growth than you had hoped; it is to be expected that your friendship will not suffer. There are advantages to doing business with good friends in that they generally are people you trust who would look out for your best interest to an even greater extent than would another professional in the same field. As long as you don't expect special rates or favors, and as long as your friend is someone whose judgment and professionalism you respect, the relationship can be strengthened and mutually beneficial. Should something go wrong, you and the friend have to separate business from friendship in analyzing the situation and not react personally. If you can keep the two separate, then a business involvement with a friend can be most satisfactory.

If your friend is someone whose company you enjoy but whose professional qualifications you question, then thank her and tell her that you are satisfied with your arrangements at this time and don't want to make a change. You can add that you will keep her offer in mind for the future.

Q. Several years ago my office was quite small and we celebrated one another's birthdays and other special occasions. Since then, the office has grown and the special occasions have gotten out of hand. It seems like almost every week someone is collecting for a birthday gift, funeral flowers, new baby gifts, or wedding gifts. It is getting too expensive, yet no one wants to hurt anyone's feelings by saying "no." Have you any advice?
A. Discuss the creation of a yearly department "kitty" where everyone chips in a set amount at the beginning of the year, to be allocated as need arises.

Guidelines should be established at the same time. The group might decide for example, that get well flowers would be sent to an employee who was in the hospital, and to his or her spouse, but not to his or her mother or great aunt. Or the group might decide that a birthday card would be purchased and signed by all for co-workers, but that birthday gifts, which would deplete the kitty rapidly, would not be given.

Q. Is there a non-offensive way to tell a co-worker that his body odor is offensive? Is it better to say nothing?
A. If you were the one who had the problem, wouldn't you want to know? As hard as it may seem, it is always a kindness to tell someone when his fly is open, that her blouse is unbuttoned, or that there is a piece of lettuce caught between his two front teeth. It is also a kindness to let someone know that his fragrance is pungent, to say the least. How to do this depends on the person. If it is a man and you are a woman, you might ask a male co-worker to take him aside and mention that his deodorant seems to not be working. Vice versa if it is a woman and you are a man. If there is a department manager whom you trust not to say "Judy tells me that your body odor is offensive..." but who rather would say "It has come to my attention that..." you can ask the manager to deal with this situation. If you are the manager or if there is no one else to deliver the message, don't make it a big deal. This kindness need not be confrontational—saying, "Whoops, Bill, better zip up!" is momentarily embarrassing, but not permanently humiliating. Saying, "Gee, Bob, it smells

like a gym locker in here! Do us both a favor and try a different brand of deodorant!" is light, breezy, and should suffice to get Bob hastening to the pharmacy. If it doesn't, in a few days say, "Hey, Bob, I guess you haven't had time to change brands of deodorant yet. Any chance of this happening soon?" Of course, this is said privately when no one else is within hearing.

Q. A car pool is required at my company, and it is a real nightmare because so many people aren't responsible about showing up on time or being ready when they are picked up. This may seem like a tactical problem, but I think it is an etiquette problem, too. It is simply rude to make others late to work. Do you agree?
A. Yes, I do. This will be an increasing problem as government regulations to decrease air pollution affect commuting habits. Some corporations are trying to assist by connecting those who live near one another, but if everyone in a car pool does not feel the same way about establishing and keeping schedules, it is a problem. This is a time when being nice is not enough. You have the right to say, "Harry, you have to be ready on time from now on—you are making us all late at least three days a week." If the car pool is more than just you and Harry, you may even have to threaten. "Harry, if you can't be on time, you'll have to find another car pool. The rest of us can't afford to be late so regularly." This is not rude on your part. While carpooling may be mandated, your choice of travel mates is not and Harry has to respect the rights and carry the responsibilities of "membership."

Table Manners

Q. *Can you suggest any "do's" and "don't's" for dining?*

A. Consideration for others is the rule governing good table manners. Don't let anyone see what you have in your mouth or make noises while eating. Avoid making a mess of the food on your plate. When cutting meat keep your elbows at your side or you risk poking your neighbor. Try not to scrape or drag chairs, rattle knives and forks against the plate, or make other unnecessary noises that can annoy those seated nearby. Do attempt to make pleasant conversation with your dining companions. In addition, there are other "don't's" everyone should try and avoid:

Don't encircle your plate with your arm.

Don't push your plate back when finished.

Don't lean back and announce "I'm through" or "I'm stuffed." Putting your utensils down across your plate shows that you have finished.

Don't put liquid in your mouth if it is already filled with food.

Don't crook your finger when picking up a cup or glass. It's an affected mannerism.

Don't ever leave your spoon in your cup, soup bowl, or in a stemmed glass.

Don't cut up your entire meal before you start to eat. Cut only one or two bites at a time.

Don't take huge mouthfuls of anything.

Don't leave half the food on your spoon or fork. Learn to put less on and then eat it in one bite.

Don't wear an excessive amount of lipstick to the table. Not only can it stain napkins, but it also looks unattractive on the rims of cups and glasses or on the silver.

Don't wipe off the tableware in a restaurant. If your silverware is dirty, ask the waiter or waitress for a clean one.

Q. *When dining "family style" do you use the same table manners as when dining in a restaurant?*
A. The same table manners apply, although the environment is less formal. The dining table, by necessity, is often in a dining alcove or the kitchen. A pretty cloth or place mats should be used. A centerpiece, although not necessary, is pleasing, and can be arranged by children, to give them a way to participate and to recognize the importance of household appointments.

Q. *Does the table setting for a family dinner differ from the table setting when guests join the family for dinner?*

A. The main difference between a table setting for guests and a table setting for family is that for the latter a minimum of utensils and plates is put at each place setting. Butter plates and knives are often omitted for family dinners, and the bread and butter are placed at the edge of the dinner plate, for example. What is important is that good manners are practiced, as well as graciousness and consideration for others—be they family or guests.

Q. What is the proper way to sit at a dinner table?
A. Ideal posture is to sit straight, but not stiffly, against the back of the chair. Hands, when one is not actually eating, may be in the lap. Tipping back one's chair is dangerous to both diner and chair.

Q. How is the table set for . . .
. . . a formal meal?
A. There is only one rule for a formal table and that is that everything must be geometrically spaced—the centerpiece in the actual center, the places at equal distances, and all utensils balanced.

A formal place setting consists of:

- Service plate, positioned so the pattern "picture" faces the diner
- Butter plate, placed above the forks at the left of the place setting
- Wineglasses, positioned according to size
- Salad fork, placed directly to the left of the

plate, assuming salad is served with or after the entrée (if salad is served as a first course, the salad fork is placed to the left of the dinner fork)

- Meat fork, positioned to the left of the salad fork

- Fish fork, positioned to the left of the meat fork. Since it is used first, it is farthest from the plate.

- Salad knife, just to the right of the plate (as noted above, the knife would go to the right of the dinner knife if salad is served first)

- Meat knife, placed to the right of the salad knife

- Fish knife, positioned to the right of the meat knife

- Butter knife, positioned diagonally at the top of the butter plate

- Soup spoon and/or fruit spoon placed outside the knives

- Oyster fork, if shellfish is to be served, beyond the spoons. This is the only fork ever placed on the right.

- Napkin

No more than three of any one implement are ever placed on the table (with the exception of the use of an oyster fork making four forks). If more than three courses are served before dessert, therefore, the fork for the fourth course is brought in with the course; or the salad fork and knife may be omitted in the beginning and brought in when salad is served.

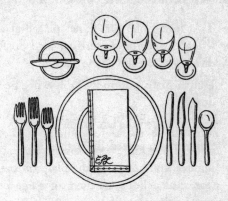

Dessert spoons and forks are brought in on the dessert plate just before dessert is served.

Q. . . . a less formal meal?
A. As at a formal dinner, everything on the table should be symmetrically and evenly spaced. Otherwise, you have much more latitude in planning an informal, casual, or semiformal dinner than you do for a formal dinner. You may use color in your table linens or other table appointments. Candles are used, just as they are on formal dinner tables, but usually as single candles rather than candelabra. They may be of any color that complements your table setting, but they must be high or low enough so that the flame is not at the eye level of the diners.

For an informal place setting, there is less of everything. There are fewer courses served, so fewer pieces of silver are set out. The typical place setting for an informal, three-course dinner includes:

- Two forks, one for dinner placed at the far left and one for dessert or salad positioned directly to the left of the plate

- Dinner plate, not on the table when guests sit down

- Salad plate, to the left of the forks

- Butter plate, placed above the forks

- Dinner knife, next to the plate on the right (for steak, chops, chicken, or game birds it may be a steak knife)

- Butter knife, placed diagonally across the butter plate

- Two spoons, a dessert spoon positioned to the right of the knife, and if soup is to be served, a soup spoon to the right of the dessert spoon

- Water goblet, placed above the knife

- Wineglass, positioned slightly forward of and to the right of the water goblet

- Napkin, may be placed either in the center of the placesetting or, if there is no salad plate, to the left of the forks

Service plates are not used at an informal dinner,

except in an appropriate size and style under a stemmed glass used for shrimp cocktail, fruit cup, etc., and under soup plates.

The dinner plate should not be on the table when you sit down, assuming you wish it to be warm when the food is served.

If you plan to serve coffee with the meal, the cup and saucer go to the right of the setting, with the coffee spoon on the table at the right of or on the saucer.

Q. . . . a family-style meal?
A. Practicality is the keynote in setting the table for family meals. A minimum number of utensils is put at each place—only those absolutely necessary. Since there is usually only one course and dessert, there may be only three pieces of silver—a fork, a knife, and a spoon for the dessert. Of course if you are having soup or fruit first, utensils for those foods must be

added. It is not necessary to have separate salad forks, although individual salad bowls should be set out.

Frozen dinners should not be eaten from the containers, but should be spooned out onto warm plates.

Ketchup, jellies, pickles, etc., may be served in their jars if no guests are present. The jars should be on saucers, and each should have its own separate serving spoon or fork on the saucer. Paper napkins are perfectly correct for family meals. However, if you prefer cloth napkins, you may wish to conserve on your laundry by using napkin rings. Each family member has his own ring. He folds his napkin at the end of the meal and puts it back in the ring, which is removed from the table until the next meal. Napkins should be changed after two or three meals.

Since no china or silver that will not be used need be placed on the table, the following setting may be used, according to your menu:

- Dinner fork at the left of the plate
- Dinner knife at the right of the plate, then the soup spoon or the oyster fork or the dessert spoon on the outside
- Glass or goblet for a beverage at the right above the knife
- Butter plate, if used, to the left and above the fork, with the butter knife laid on it diagonally from the upper left to the lower right
- Salad plate at the left of the fork

- Napkin at the left or in the center of the setting
- Coffee mug or cup and saucer with a spoon at the right

If the food is to be passed, the warm dinner plates are at each place on the table when the family sits down, or they are stacked in front of the head of the household if he or she is to serve. Often plates are served directly from the stove in order to avoid the use of extra platters and serving dishes.

Q. *What should a guest do when dining with a family of another faith who say grace before meals, sit quietly or join in?*

A. A guest certainly may join in if he or she feels comfortable doing so. If your hosts ask you to join hands during the prayer this is simply a gesture of loving friendship and in no way means you are worshiping their faith by doing so. However, it is not necessary for guests to cross themselves, even though their Catholic hosts do so—nor to make any gesture not practiced in their own faith. If a guest chooses not to join in grace, he or she may sit (or stand) quietly until grace is finished. A clue as to whether grace is to be said is whether the hostess immediately puts her napkin in her lap. If she does not, it is a signal that she may be waiting to say grace as soon as everyone is silent.

Q. What is the proper way to handle a napkin at dinner?
A. Ordinarily, as soon as you are seated you put your napkin in your lap. At a formal dinner, however, you wait for your hostess to put hers on her lap first. Remove the napkin from the table, place it on your lap, and unfold it as much as necessary. Never tuck it in to your collar, belt, or between buttons of a shirt. When using your napkin, blot or pat your lips— never wipe with it as if it were a washcloth.

When the meal is finished, or if you leave the table during the meal, put the napkin on the left side of your place, or if the plates have been removed, in the center. It should not be crumpled up, nor should it be refolded; rather, it is laid on the table in loose folds so that it does not spread itself out. At a formal dinner party, the hostess lays her napkin on the table as a signal that the meal is over, and the guests then lay their napkins on the table—not before.

Q. How do I know when to start eating as a guest at dinner?
A. It is incumbent upon the host or hostess to ask

guests to begin a hot course after three or four people have been served. This keeps the food of those who have been served first from getting cold. Although most of us have been raised to wait for the hostess to "lift her fork" before starting, this is true only for a first course and for dessert. For a hot entrée, if she forgets to encourage guests to begin, it is not incorrect for them to start eating after three or four have been served.

Q. Which glasses are used for which wines? Where are the glasses placed?
A. Sherry, which is served at room temperature, is poured into small, V-shaped glasses.

Sherry

White wine, which is served well chilled, is poured into round-bowled, stemmed glasses.

German   Alsace
White Wine Glasses

Red wine, which is served at room temperature, is poured into less rounded, more tulip-shaped glasses that are narrower at the rim than are white wine glasses.

Bordeaux   Burgundy

Champagne, which is served very well chilled, is poured into either flat, wide-rimmed glasses or into champagne flutes—stemmed glasses that are long and narrow.

Coupe   Flute

Wine glasses are placed on the table according to size so that the smaller ones are not hidden behind the larger ones.

The water goblet is placed directly above the knives at the right of the plates.

The champagne glass is next to it at a slight distance to the right.

The claret or red wine glass or the white wine

glass is positioned in front of and between the water goblet and champagne glass.

The sherry glass is placed either to the right or in front of the wineglass.

Rather than grouping the wineglasses, you may place them in a straight row slanting downward from the water goblet at the upper left to the sherry glass at the lower right.

Q. *Is it correct to reach for something—a serving dish, for instance—across the table?*
A. No, it is never correct to reach across the table. It

is correct to reach for anything that does not necessitate stretching across your neighbor or leaning far across the table yourself. If the item you want is not close at hand, simply ask the person nearest to it, "Would you please pass the butter, George?"

Q. When someone asks you to "pass the salt" should you pass the pepper too?
A. It is okay to pass both the salt and pepper when someone says "Please pass the salt." However, there is *no* rule about it and it is perfectly correct to simply pass the one that was requested.

Q. May a dinner guest ask the hostess for an item that does not appear on the table, such as mustard when ham is served?
A. Yes, it is correct if an accompaniment that is ordinarily served is missing, probably because of an oversight. You should not, however, ask for anything unusual that your hostess might not have.

Q. How should guests serve themselves at a family-style dinner?
A. Anything served on a piece of toast, with the exception of game birds, should be lifted from the platter on the toast. The toast with its topping is lifted with the spoon and held in place with the fork. If you don't want to eat the toast, simply put it to one side of your plate.

Gravy should be put *on* the meat, potatoes, or rice and condiments at the side of whatever they accompany. Olives, nuts, radishes, or celery are put on the bread-and-butter plate if there is one, otherwise on the edge of the plate from which one is eating.

When a serving dish is passed around the table for each guest to help himself, it is passed counterclockwise. Each person helps himself and then may offer to hold the dish for the next person.

Q. *May I refuse a dish at dinner I dislike?*
A. If you are among friends, you may refuse with a polite "No, thank you." Otherwise it is good manners to take at least a little of every dish that is offered to you and eat it. You need not give your reason for refusing a dish, but if it is because of an allergy, diet, or other physical cause, you may quietly explain to your hostess without drawing the attention of the entire table. When declining a dish offered by a waiter, say "No, thank you," quietly. At a buffet dinner you need only help yourself to those dishes that appeal to you.

Q. *How do you know with which piece of flatware to begin eating?*
A. It's easy! You always start with the implement of each type that is farthest from the plate. There is only one exception to this rule. If the table is incorrectly set and you realize it, you must choose the implement that is appropriate. For example, if the small shellfish fork has been put next to the plate, you would not use the big dinner fork for the shrimp cocktail and leave the little fork for the entrée, even though they were placed in that order.

Q. What is the proper way to use a knife and fork?
A. The American custom of "zigzag" eating (changing the fork from the left to the right hand after cutting) is perfectly correct. The knife is put down on the plate after cutting and the fork is raised to the mouth, tines up.

Equally correct is the European method of leaving the fork in the left hand after cutting and raising it to the mouth in the same position in which it was held for cutting, tines down.

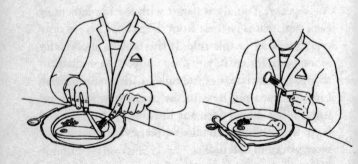

The knife may also be used as a "pusher," if necessary. It is held in the left hand in the same position as when cutting with the right hand, and the tip of the blade helps to guide and push the food onto the fork.

When the main course is finished, the knife and fork are placed beside each other on the dinner plate diagonally from upper left to lower right, the handles extended slightly over the edge of the plate. The dessert spoon and/or fork is placed in the same position. If dessert is served in a stemmed or deep bowl on another plate, the dessert spoon is put down on the plate, never left in the bowl. If the bowl is shallow and wide, the spoon may be left in it, or on the plate below it, as you wish.

Q. How should you . . .
. . . eat dessert?
A. Dessert may be eaten with a spoon or fork or both. Stewed fruit is held in place with the fork and cut and eaten with the spoon. Peaches or other juicy fruits are peeled and then eaten with knife and fork, but dry fruits, such as apples, may be cut and then eaten with the fingers.

Pie is eaten with a fork; if it is à la mode, the spoon is also used.

Ice cream is generally eaten with a spoon, but when accompanied by cake, either the spoon alone or both the spoon and fork may be used.

If you cannot eat a dessert, no matter what it is—whether plum, Napoleon, or cream puff—without getting it all over your fingers, you must use a fork and, when necessary, a spoon or a knife also.

Q. . . . eat soups?
A. Either clear soup or thick soup may be served in a cup with one handle or with handles on both sides. After taking a spoonful or two you may pick up the cup if the soup is cool enough, or continue to use your spoon if you prefer.

Clear soups are sometimes served in a shallow soup plate. When the level of the soup is so low that you must tip the plate to avoid scraping the bottom, lift the near edge and tip the plate away from you, never toward you. Spoon the soup either away from you or toward you, whichever is less awkward.

Both soup cups and soup plates should be served with a saucer or a plate beneath them. The spoon, when not in use or when the soup is finished, is laid on the saucer when a soup cup is used, but is left in the soup plate rather than on the plate under it.

Q. . . . eat bread and butter?
A. Bread should be broken with the fingers into moderate-sized pieces, not necessarily single-mouthful bits. To butter bread, hold a piece on the edge of the bread-and-butter plate or the place plate. With a butter knife, spread enough butter on it for a mouthful or two at a time. If there is no butter knife, use any other knife you find available, taking care not to smear food particles from the knife onto the butter.

Common-sense exceptions are hot biscuits or toast which can be buttered all over immediately, since they are most delicious when the butter is melted. No bread, however, should be held flat on the palm of the hand and buttered with the hand held in the air.

Q. . . . eat salad?
A. If large leaves of lettuce or large chunks of salad vegetables are in the salad, they may be cut with a knife and fork into small, manageable pieces before being eaten. This is preferable to attempting to roll large lettuce leaves around the tines of the fork; if they let go they shoot salad dressing all over you, the table, and your neighbors.

Q. . . . drink hot beverages?
A. When hot coffee, chocolate, or tea is served in a mug instead of in a cup and saucer, the problem arises of what to do with the spoon—which should never be left in the mug. The solution depends somewhat on the table covering. If the placemats or tablecloth are paper or plastic, the spoon may be wiped clean with the lips

and laid beside the mug. If the mats or cloth are fabric, the bowl of the spoon, face down, should be rested on the edge of the butter plate or dinner plate, with the spoon handle on the table. You may ask for a dish on which to place a tea bag (after pressing out excess liquid against the side of the mug with a spoon) or put it on the edge of the butter or dinner plate.

When hot beverages are served in a cup with a saucer, the spoon is placed at the side of the saucer, as is a tea bag. When the beverage slops into the saucer, the best course is to replace the saucer with a clean one. If this is not possible, rather than drip coffee each time you lift the cup to your mouth, it is permissible to pour the liquid back into the cup and use a paper napkin to dry the bottom of the cup.

Beverages that are too hot to drink may be sipped, never slurped, from a spoon.

Q. . . . drink iced tea or coffee?
A. Preferably, iced tea and coffee are served in a glass placed on a saucer or coaster. The saucer, then, is the place to put the iced tea spoon. Otherwise, the spoon may be rested as a spoon served with a mug of coffee or tea, described above.

Q. . . . use salt in a saltcellar?
A. If there is no spoon in a saltcellar (a tiny, open bowl), use the tip of a clean knife. If the saltcellar is for you alone, you also may take a pinch with your fingers. Salt that is to be dipped into should be put on the bread-and-butter plate or on the rim of whatever

plate is in front of you. Food should be salted only after it has been tasted, never before.

Q. . . . *handle food that is too hot or spoiled?*
A. If a bite of food is too hot, quickly take a swallow of water. Only if there is no beverage at all, and your mouth is scalding, should you spit it out. It should be removed onto your fork or into your fingers and quickly put on the edge of the plate. Spoiled food should not be swallowed but removed as quickly and as unobtrusively as possible, also with fork or fingers. To spit anything whatever into a napkin is unnecessary and not permissible.

Q. *What do you do when . . .*
. . . you begin choking on meat or bones?
A. If a sip of water does not help but a good cough will, cover your mouth with your napkin and cough. Remove the abrasive morsel with your fingers and put it on the edge of your plate. If you continue to cough, excuse yourself from the table. In the event that you are really choking, you will be unable to speak. Don't hesitate to get someone's attention to help you. The seriousness of your condition will quickly be recognized, and it is no time to worry about manners. Keeping calm and acting quickly might well save your life.

Q. . . . *you need to cough, sneeze, or blow your nose?*
A. Cover your mouth and nose with your handkerchief or, if you have no handkerchief, with your nap-

kin. In an emergency, your hand will do better than nothing at all. It is not necessary to leave the table to perform these functions unless the bout turns out to be prolonged. In that case, you should excuse yourself until the seizure has passed. You also should excuse yourself if you have no handkerchief or tissue and need to blow your nose. Never use your napkin to blow your nose.

Q. . . . discover stones, bugs, or hair in your food?
A. If it is not too upsetting to you, remove the object without calling attention to it and go on eating. If you are truly repulsed, leave the dish untouched rather than embarrass your hostess in a private home. At a restaurant you may—and should—point out the error to your waiter and ask for a replacement. If the alien object has reached your mouth without your previously noticing it, remove it with your fingers as inconspicuously as possible and place it at the edge of your plate.

Q. . . . get food stuck in a tooth?
A. It is not permissible to use a toothpick or to use your fingers to pick at your teeth when at the table. If something stuck in your tooth actually is hurting, excuse yourself from the table and go to the bathroom to remove it. Otherwise, wait until the end of the meal and then go take care of it, asking for a toothpick if necessary.

Q. . . . spill something?

A. Pick up jelly, a bit of vegetable, or other solid food with the blade of your knife or a clean spoon. If it has caused a stain, and you are at someone's house, dab a little water from your glass on it with the corner of your napkin. Apologize to your hostess, who, in turn, should not add to your embarrassment by calling attention to the accident.

If you spill wine or water at a formal dinner or in a restaurant, try quietly to attract the attention of the butler or waiter, who will bring a cloth to cover the spot. At an informal dinner without servants, offer to get a cloth or sponge to mop up the liquid and help the hostess clean up in any way you can.

Q. In whose name are reservations made?
A. Reservations are usually made in one name only. They are made in the name of the host or hostess who is giving the dinner party or, if a group of friends plan to meet at a restaurant and each will pay for his own meal, the reservation may be made in the name of the person who is delegated to make it, or in the name of anyone else in the group.

Q. Why are men's coats checked but women's are not?
A. Often checkrooms are so small that the attendants will not accept a woman's coat. Other checkrooms will not check a fur coat because the management doesn't want to be responsible for it. Generally, a woman wears her coat until she is seated and then removes it, throwing the shoulders back over her chair. A woman may, however, check her coat.

Q. Who leads the way to the table, the man or the woman?

A. Women generally walk behind the headwaiter, and the men follow them. But if a man is giving a dinner for six or more, the women would have to wait at the table until told by their host where to sit. In this case it causes less confusion if he goes in ahead of his guests. When a couple are hosts, the woman seats the guests, usually going first with the most important lady, and the host follows last.

Q. When a couple is dining at a restaurant with a view who gets the better seat?

A. The woman is given the better seat, unless for some reason she prefers another seat. In this case she stands beside the other chair saying, "I'd rather sit here if I may."

Q. If several people are meeting at a restaurant does the first arriving diner take a table or wait for the others?

A. The first arrival should wait for the second rather than go in and sit alone, unless the first arrival sees that the restaurant is filling up and there may shortly be no tables left. When two arrive together they should ask to be seated, explaining to the headwaiter that others are joining them and asking him to see that they are directed to the table. This avoids over-crowding the entry and sometimes is the only way of holding a reservation. Some restaurants, however, will not seat a group until all members are present.

Q. Who gives the order to the waiter? I thought the woman was supposed to tell her choice to the gentleman with whom she was dining and he conveyed it to the waiter. Is this still done?

A. You are correct in that, for many years, a woman, when dining with a man, never spoke to the waiter herself. This rule is outdated and it is perfectly correct for a woman, particularly when there are more than two people in the party, to give her order directly to the waiter. When the waiter looks straight at a woman and asks, "What kind of dressing would you like on your salad?" it is insulting if she turns away and relays her order through her escort. Many waiters ask the woman for her order first in an effort to be polite, and there is no reason why she should not answer directly.

Q. On a restaurant menu what do table d'hôte and à la carte mean?

A. Table d'hôte means a set price for a complete meal, irrespective of how many courses are offered. "Club" breakfasts and lunches, "blue plate" dinners, or any meals at fixed prices are table d'hôte. Usually, choices of an appetizer or soup, an entrée with vegetables, salad, dessert, and coffee are included in the one price.

Another type of table d'hôte menu is one that has a price beside each entrée. This price varies, with beef, for example, costing more than chicken, but includes the full range of courses at that price. Sometimes a table d'hôte menu will show a price after a particular item, noting, for example, "shrimp cocktail, $3.00

extra." This means the full meal is included in the fixed price, plus the additional amount if shrimp cocktail is ordered instead of an appetizer that does not have its own price.

À la carte means that you order from a list of dishes and you pay the price listed beside each dish— even for your vegetable, salad, and coffee.

Very often a separate card or a box insert on the à la carte menu reads "Special dinner $22.00" or whatever the price may be, so that you can order the special for that price, but that any item taken from the regular bill of fare will be charged for as an extra.

Usually it is easy to know which is which because a price follows each item on an à la carte menu while the prices are listed only by the entrée or at the top of a table d'hôte menu.

Q. *How do restaurant table manners differ from the manners one uses at home?*
A. Although table manners are much the same whether you are eating at home or at a restaurant, there are a few special problems that do arise when dining out.

When vegetables and potatoes are served in individual side dishes, you may eat them directly from the small dishes or you may put them on your dinner plate by using a serving spoon or sliding them directly out of the small dish. You may ask the waiter to remove the empty dishes, thus avoiding an overcrowded table.

You certainly may eat the olives, cherries, or onions served in cocktails, if you wish. If there is no pick, wait until you have drunk enough so you will not wet your fingers and lift out the trimming and eat it with your fingers. Slices of oranges in old-fashioneds are not usually eaten as it is too messy to chew the pulp off the rind.

When an uncut loaf of bread is placed on the table the host slices or breaks off two or three individual portions and offers them with the rest of the loaf in the breadbasket or on the plate to the people beside him. This is then passed around the table, and each man should cut or break off a portion for himself and the woman next to him.

If coffee or tea is placed on the table without first having been poured by the waiter, the person nearest the pot should offer to pour, filling his or her own cup last.

If sugar, crackers, cream, or other accompaniments to meals are served with paper wrappers or in plastic or cardboard containers, the wrappers should be crumpled up tightly and either tucked under the rim of your plate or placed on the edge of the saucer or butter plate. Do not put them in the ashtray if there are smokers present, since their lighted cigarettes could easily set the paper on fire.

When jelly or marmalade is served in a plastic or paper container it should be taken out with the butter knife (or dinner knife if there is no butter knife) and put on the bread-and-butter plate. The top is put back in the empty container, which is left on the table beside the butter plate.

Q. How do you summon the waiter?
A. In the United States, the usual way is to catch his eye and then raise your hand, first finger pointing up, as if to say "attention" or "listen." If he does not look in your direction you may call "Waiter" (or "Waitress") quietly, or if he is too far away to hear you, ask any other waiter nearby, "Please call our waiter." "Miss" is also a correct term for a waitress, but "Sir" is not correct for a waiter, whether used by a woman, man, or a youngster.

Q. After finishing dinner at a restaurant may I freshen my lipstick at the table?
A. Yes, you may put on lipstick or quickly powder your nose, but to look in a mirror and daub at your face for any length of time is bad manners. Worse yet is to comb or brush your hair at a restaurant table or in any public place. Never fuss with, fix or touch your hair in any place where food is served. This applies to both men and women.

Q. When dining at a restaurant and discovering friends are also dining there is it permissible to stop by their table for a moment to say hello?
A. Yes, but just for a moment. If you wish a longer conversation, it is best to arrange to meet later, rather than crowd the restaurant aisle and interrupt your friends' meal, not to mention causing them to

stand for any length of time in order to be polite.

All men at a small table rise when a woman is being introduced, as they do whenever a woman stops to talk. When a group is large only those closest to the visitor rise. If a woman stopping at a table is introduced to other women seated there, the latter never rise—even though they be young and the visitor older.

All the men at the table do not rise when another man stops on his way by. When someone comes up to speak to one of the diners, that man only should rise to shake hands. The visitor should then ask him to please be seated and finish what he has to say.

When a man is seated at a banquet and someone—man or woman—stops by to say "Hello," he merely nods and extends his hand. If he rose either he would get cramps from the crouched position or he would upset the table trying to straighten up, but he may apologize for not rising.

Q. *Most restaurants serve more food than I can eat comfortably at one sitting. May I ask for a doggy bag to bring the food home?*
A. Yes, you may. It is perfectly acceptable if you are comfortable asking and if your portion is just too large for you to finish at the restaurant.

Q. *How do you complain about restaurant service? Do you speak with the server or ask for the manager?*
A. Complaints should be made quietly, without making a fuss or attracting the attention of other diners.

They should be made first to the waiter (or the person who commits the error), and if he or she makes no effort to correct the situation, the headwaiter or whoever is in charge of the dining room should be notified. Think twice when your complaint is about laziness or inattention, however, to be sure it is not the waiter's inability to serve too many people. Often the tables are poorly allotted or another waiter is absent and although your waiter is working as hard as he can, he still cannot keep up with the requests of the patrons. It is correct to complain to the manager, but be careful not to put the blame on the waiter who is no happier about the situation than you are. Otherwise, rudeness and laziness should be reported, meat that is not done as you requested should be replaced, and food that is cold should be taken back and reheated.

If, after making a legitimate complaint, you receive no satisfaction from anyone, you may reduce the tip or leave none at all, and avoid that restaurant in the future.

On the other hand, appreciative comments are more than welcome and offered all too infrequently. If your meal and the service were excellent, it is extremely thoughtful to say so, both to the waiter and manager.

Q. How does one host a dinner at a restaurant?
A. A thoughtful host selects a restaurant he thinks his guest or guests will enjoy and reserves a table. If the host has ordered the dinner ahead of time he or she must try to check the dishes ahead or as they are served

to make sure that everything is as requested. If dinner has not been ordered ahead of time, it is the host's duty to take the guest's order and give it to the waiter, or if the party is large, to make sure that the waiter gets the order correctly from each person. In either case, if there are mistakes the host must tactfully and politely see that they are corrected, without embarrassing the guests.

When paying the check, the host does not display the total but puts the money (or the signed credit card form) quietly on the plate and nods to the waiter to remove it. The host indicates to his guests that it is time to leave by rising or with a remark. If the head-waiter has been especially helpful, the host unobtrusively slips a tip (from five dollars depending on the size of the group) into his hand and thanks him as the party is leaving the restaurant.

Q. Does dining at a smorgasbord, cafeteria-style, or oriental restaurant differ from dining at a restaurant with full table service?
A. Yes, each is different in several aspects. At a smorgasbord restaurant, individual tables are set as usual, but the meal is not served by waiters. Instead it is set up as a buffet with stacks of small plates at one end to be filled with reasonable amounts of food. Since you are expected to make as many trips as you wish from your seat to the smorgasbord and back, you should never overload your plate and you should only choose foods that go well together each time you serve yourself. Leave your used plate and silver at your table for the waiter to remove while you are

helping yourself to your next selection. Start with fish, followed by cold cuts and salad, then by cheeses and a bit of fresh fruit, if you wish. You then choose your hot food, and end with dessert and coffee. It is intended that you take your time to enjoy your dinner. When you are finished, it is expected that you leave your waiter a tip.

A cafeteria is more informal than a smorgasbord. Like a smorgasbord, you serve yourself or are served as you walk through the buffet setup, selecting your complete meal. You pay for your meal at the end of the cafeteria line. Unlike a smorgasbord, if you go back for something else, you again pay for your selection. When the restaurant is crowded and there are no empty tables, it is perfectly all right to take an empty chair at an occupied table, but it is polite to first ask, "Is this seat taken?" or "Do you mind if I sit here?" When there are busboys who carry the trays to the tables, they are generally given a tip of a quarter or fifty cents depending on the cafeteria and the amount of food on the tray. Diners who join strangers at a table are under no obligation to talk to them, but it is polite to respond if he or she speaks to them, and all right to speak first if the other person seems receptive.

Oriental restaurants are like full table service restaurants with the exception in Chinese restaurants that serving dishes are placed in the center of the table so that diners may sample each rather than limit themselves to just one entrée. Some Japanese restaurants request that diners remove their shoes, and some have low tables at which diners sit on cushions on the floor or in a recessed area. If this is uncomfort-able or unappealing, most also have regular tables available. Although chopsticks often are set at each place instead of silver, it is perfectly all right to request a knife and a fork.

In Houses of Worship

Q. Is it proper to ask a priest for his blessing, perhaps as you are about to leave his company? May a person of another faith ask a priest's blessing?
A. It is perfectly correct for a Catholic to ask for a priest's blessing. It is also permissible for other Christians to ask for a blessing, since they worship the same God.

Q. My neighbor, who is Jewish, has asked me to attend services with her and then attend a Passover Seder. I would love to do this, but I am clueless as to what is expected of me and what I could offer toward the Seder and don't want to appear rude out of ignorance. What should I do?
A. It cannot be said enough times that clear communication is one of the basic tenets on which etiquette is based. Just ask her. Tell her how much you are looking forward to joining her and learning more about her faith and customs, but that you don't know what to do. Ask what you could bring to the Seder and what you could read or study ahead of time to help you participate more fully. This is not impolite, but shows

genuine interest and caring which is characteristic of a thoughtful friend.

Q. Some close family members have recently converted to a different religion and they are determined to convert us, too. This is making family get-togethers uncomfortable. We are perfectly happy with our religious affiliation, feel just as religious as they do, and resent their constant attempts to proselytize and implications that we will not be "saved" until we join them in their new church. We hate to sever the relationship since our family isn't all that big to begin with, but just what can we say without being outright rude?

A. There is no one as dedicated as a recent convert, so you must be just as emphatic as your relatives in stating that you are happy with your affiliation. Say that you respect their choice and are happy for them, and that you expect the same respect from them. If their zeal continues, you must say that you have listened to them and appreciate their strong feelings, but that you are not the least bit interested in converting. Tell them you are interested in maintaining a close relationship and hope they will help keep these ties strong by expressing interest in other aspects of your lives and theirs.

Q. How should you dress for a service at a church? A synagogue?

A. Although clothing restrictions have been greatly relaxed in recent years, the correct dress is still conservative. Even today skirts or conservative pants and jackets for women and suits, slacks, and shirts and/or sport jackets for men are preferable to jeans or shorts for conventional church or synagogue services.

Hats for women are no longer required in any of the Christian churches, but are always correct. In Orthodox Jewish synagogues married women are required to wear a head covering.

Men never wear hats in Christian churches—they always do in synagogues. If you are not Jewish and are attending a synagogue for a service, a wedding, or a funeral, there are extra yarmulkes by the entrance. Although it is not your faith or practice, it is expected that you wear a yarmulke or hat when attending a service.

Q. Do ushers escort everyone to their seats in church?
A. Not necessarily. Often ushers simply greet worshipers as they enter and let them seat themselves. If the ushers do seat members of the congregation, they escort them to a pew. A woman does not take the usher's arm unless she needs assistance, but rather follows him as he leads the way to a vacant seat. The usher stands aside while the arrival—whether single or a couple—steps in. Women precede their husbands into the pew, going in far enough to allow room for him—and for children or others who are with them. At a special service, such as a wedding or first communion, early arrivals may keep their aisle seats, standing to let later arrivals get past them. At weekly services, however, those who are already in the pews should move over to make room for later arrivals.

Q. *Is it acceptable to stop and chat or wave to friends before services begin?*

A. It is perfectly correct to nod, smile, or wave at acquaintances before a service starts, and if a friend sits down next to you or in front of you, you may certainly lean over and whisper "Hello." You should not, however, chat, carry on a prolonged conversation, or introduce people to one another until after the service.

Q. *If you decide to attend another place of worship on a regular basis do you owe the clergyman an explanation?*

A. Yes, you owe the clergyman or clergywoman of your former church or synagogue an explanation, both for record-keeping and personal reasons. In some denominations each parish is assessed according to the number of registered members, and therefore its financial condition can be harmed if a member who leaves is still enrolled but not contributing.

You owe the clergyman or clergywoman a personal explanation of your reasons for leaving, either by letter or in person. Although it may be difficult, try to be very honest and clear. While he or she may be hurt or upset, your comments may help him to serve the congregation better.

Q. *To me, any house of worship should be a place of quiet for meditation and prayer. There are a few families in my church who appear to be oblivious to their children and let them talk, thump their feet against* *the pew, and play with noisy toys. I went up to them one morning and asked them to keep their children quiet. They were quite offended and don't come to church anymore. The minister is annoyed with me. Was I wrong?*

A. You are correct that it is inconsiderate of parents to permit their children to disrupt an entire congregation's attempt to worship. A different way to handle this situation would be to make an appointment to speak with the minister and ask him or her to speak privately to the parents about the problem of noise and disruption. Many churches offer a nursery during worship for just this reason. It is difficult for small children to remain quiet for the length of time most services take, and a nursery allows them more freedom to release some of their energy. It is really the minister's responsibility to periodically announce that nursery service is available and to remind parents that while the church loves to have its children present, it would be appreciated if parents would take them outside or to the nursery if they become noisy during worship.

Q. Last week I made the mistake of again sitting in front of two women who talk through the entire service. The first time I just sat and seethed and tried to tune them out. This time I turned around and glowered at them. They now are not speaking to me. What should I have done?

A. You did not do anything wrong in confronting them with their thoughtlessness and rudeness by your look. You might initiate a conversation with them outside of the sanctuary, however, to say that you are sorry you annoyed them, but that you have very sensitive hearing and found their talking distracting. This is about all you can politely say, since a lecture or more direct criticism would serve no better purpose than a quiet comment and probably would not be well received. Naturally, you will take care not to sit near them in the future and will endeavor to be pleasant and friendly when you see them.

Q. *I occasionally attend church with a friend of another faith. Do I participate in the service?*
A. Unless some part of the service is opposed to your religious convictions, you should attempt to follow the lead of the congregation. Stand when they stand, sing when they sing, pray when they pray. If there is a part in which you do not wish to participate, sit quietly until that portion of the service is over.

A Protestant need not cross himself or genuflect when entering a pew in a Catholic church. Nor must you kneel if your custom is to pray seated—just bend forward and bow your head.

If you are taking communion in a church that is strange to you, watch what the congregation does and follow their lead.

When you attend another church you should make a contribution when the offering plate is passed. This is a way of saying "Thank you" to the church you are visiting.

At Times of
Loss and Grieving

Q. When and how are calls of condolence made?
A. They should be made as soon as possible after hearing of the death. If the friends are very close, you will probably be admitted to speak to them. If you are, you should offer your services to help in any way you can. There are countless ways to be helpful, from assisting with such needs as food and child care, to making phone calls and answering the door. If they do not need anything, you offer your sympathy and leave without delay.

A condolence call to a Jewish family is made during the seven days following the burial. This period of mourning is known as sitting *shivah* (*shivah* is the Hebrew word for seven). The call is made to the home of those in mourning and gives you an opportunity to express your sympathy to the bereaved.

When you are not well acquainted with the family and do not wish to intrude on their privacy, you may leave your card with "with deepest sympathy" written across the top.

At a funeral home you sign the register and offer the family your sympathy in person. If you do not see them, you should write a letter of sympathy at once. Telephoning is not improper, but it may cause inconvenience by tying up the line, which is always needed at these times for notifying members of the family and for making necessary arrangements.

Visits of condolence need not be returned.

Q. How should relatives be notified of a death?
A. Members of the family and other close friends should be called on the telephone. Other relatives, even those who live at some distance, should also be called, but if expense is a factor, friends who would not be attending a funeral or memorial service may be notified by letter.

Q. If the family elects to have a newspaper notice of death how is it worded?
A. Newspaper notices usually contain the date of death, names of the immediate family, hours and locations where friends may call on the family, place and time of the funeral, and frequently, a request that a contribution be given to a charity instead of flowers being sent.

The word *suddenly* is sometimes inserted immediately after the deceased's name to indicate that there had not been a long illness, or that the death was by accident. Often "after a long illness" is inserted to communicate that information.

Instead of "Friends may call at (address)" the phrase "Reposing at Memorial Funeral Home" is commonly used.

The deceased's age is not generally included unless he or she is very young or the age is needed to establish further identification.

Daughters of the deceased are listed before sons. A woman's notice always includes her given and maiden name for purposes of identification. The same is true when married daughters and sisters are mentioned.

The use of adjectives such as *beloved, loving, devoted,* etc., is optional.

A woman's notice might read:

Cohen—Helen Weinberg, on May 13. [Beloved] wife of Isaac, [loving] mother of Rebecca, Paul, and Samuel, [devoted] sister of Anna Weinberg Gold and Paul Weinberg. Services Thursday, May 14, 2:00 P.M., at Star Funeral Home, 41 Chestnut Street, Pittsburgh. In lieu of flowers, contributions may be sent to the United Jewish Appeal, or your favorite charity.

A man's notice might read:

Johnson—Michael B., on December 12, 1988. [Beloved] husband of the late Kathleen Stuart Johnson. [Devoted] father of Erin Johnson Flynn, Brad S., and Sean R. Friends may call at 44 Wendt Avenue, Harrison, New York, on Friday, December 15, 2–5. Funeral service Saturday, December

16, 11:30 A.M., St. John's Lutheran Church, Mamaroneck, New York.

An obituary may also be run. The family may submit it, but it is the option of the editors to decide whether they wish to print it or not. In the event that one is submitted, it includes the residence of family members listed (Brad S. of New York City, Sean R. of Mamaroneck) and information about the previous activities, memberships, affiliations, and career of the deceased. If the person who died was prominent in the community, it is probable that the newspapers have a file on him or her. The information they have should be checked by someone who is acquainted with the facts so that no errors will be made in the published obituary.

Q. What does "in lieu of flowers" mean?
A. It means that the family requests a contribution to a specific charity instead of flowers and believes the contribution will help them to feel that some good has come from their loss. A check is sent to the charity with a note saying "This donation is sent in memory of Mrs. Roy Haskell of 10 Stetson Way, Austin, Texas." Your address should appear on the note.

Occasionally a notice reads, "Please send a contribution to your favorite charity." You are free to choose whichever one you wish, but it is thoughtful to select one that might also mean something to the bereaved family.

The amount of the contribution is up to you. However, you should not give less than you would have paid for a flower arrangement.

If no "in lieu of" appears in the notice, you should send flowers.

Another option is to send a plant or flower arrangement to the family a few days after the funeral as an indication of your continuing sympathy and love. Sometimes friends do this instead of funeral flowers or contributions; others do it in addition to one or the other. Cards accompanying these flowers or plants should not mention the recent loss, but may simply say, "With love from us all" or "With love."

Q. What role can friends play immediately following a death?
A. In addition to helping with family meals, child care, making telephone calls, and answering the door, they can help organize food if there is to be a gathering of family and friends after the funeral. They can offer to stay at the house during the funeral service (sometimes houses are robbed during a funeral when it is known that no one will be at home) or they can offer to be in charge of flowers, collecting all the accompanying cards one hour before the service and writing a description of the flowers so a later note, from the family, can properly thank the giver, including a specific mention of the "beautiful coral roses" or the "laurel wreath with gardenias." Often this service is performed by the funeral home. If it is not, it is

a tremendous help to the family to have someone take care of it for them.

Other services friends can provide include offering to have out-of-town relatives attending the funeral stay at their homes and offering to drive family members to and from the funeral home or the church or synagogue or to run other errands.

Q. Who generally serve as pallbearers? May someone refuse to serve as a pallbearer? What are honorary pallbearers and what role do they play in a funeral?
A. Generally, close male friends of the deceased serve as pallbearers. They may be asked when they come to pay their respects, or by telephone. Members of the immediate family are never chosen, as their place is with the family.

One cannot refuse an invitation to be a pallbearer except for illness or absence from the area.

Honorary pallbearers serve only at church funerals. They do not carry the coffin. This service is performed by the assistants of the funeral director, who are expertly trained. The honorary pallbearers sit in the first pews on the left, and after the service leave the church two by two, walking immediately in front of the coffin.

Q. Who serves as ushers at a funeral or memorial service and what do they do?
A. Ushers may be chosen in addition to, or in place of, pallbearers. Although funeral directors will supply men to perform the task, it is infinitely better to select

men from the family (not immediate family) or close friends, who will recognize those who come and seat them according to their closeness to the family or according to their own wishes.

At both a funeral and a memorial service, ushers hand those who enter a bulletin of the service, if one is used, and show them to a pew. They do not offer their arms to a woman unless she needs assistance, but walk slightly ahead. At a memorial service, they also ask people to sign a register, if the family wishes, before entering.

When there are no pallbearers the ushers sit in the front pews on the left and exit ahead of the coffin as pallbearers would. If there are pallbearers the ushers remain at the back of the church.

Q. If you extend an expression of sympathy at a funeral home do you also write a condolence note?
A. A visitor who sees and personally extends his sympathy at the funeral home need not write a note of condolence, unless he wishes to write an absent member of the family. Those who merely sign the register and do not speak with family members should, in addition, write a note.

Q. Who may stop by a funeral home to pay his respects? Who attends a funeral?
A. Anyone who wishes to express his sympathy to the family of the deceased may stop by a funeral home and pay his respects. People who do not feel they are close enough to intrude on the privacy of the

bereaved may stop in at times other than those during which the family is there and sign the register.

If the newspaper notice reads "Funeral private," only those who have received an invitation from the family may go. If the hour and the location of the service are printed in the paper, that is considered an invitation to anyone who wishes to attend. All members of the family should find out when the funeral is to take place and go to it without waiting to be notified.

A divorced man or woman should go to the funeral of their former spouse if the latter had not remarried and there are children involved. Even if the deceased had remarried, the former spouse should attend if cordial relations have been maintained with the family of the deceased, although he or she should sit in the rear and not attempt to join the family. If the deceased had remarried, and there was ill feeling, the former spouse should not attend, but should send flowers and a brief note of condolence.

Q. *Can you give me some guidance on what to do when paying my respects at a funeral home?*
A. When there is a coffin present, and if you feel comfortable in doing so, you go forward to the coffin to say a prayer, either standing in front of it or kneeling on the kneeling bench usually provided. You should not stay by the coffin for a protracted period of time when there are others waiting for you to finish, nor should you rush past. You then seek close family members to offer your sympathy, talk with them for a few minutes, sign the register provided,

and depart. You may also sit quietly in chairs provided to meditate or reflect on the life of the deceased. If, as is often the case, there is active conversation among other visitors and you are seeing old friends and family members whom you have not seen for a long period, there is nothing wrong with greeting them and speaking quietly. Your conversation may be about the deceased and his or her life, although it frequently strays into other areas as those who have not seen each other in quite a while catch up on news.

No matter how "social" the gathering becomes, you should not tell jokes or talk loudly. You should not leave without expressing your sympathy directly to the family of the deceased, and you should not browse among the flowers, Mass cards, or other gifts checking to see who sent what. You may admire the flowers, of course, but you may not examine them. Your visit can be very brief, or it can be throughout the duration of visiting hours if you are a close friend or family member who can offer support and assistance with your presence.

When you depart, you may again approach the coffin to say a prayer, but you do not need to say goodbye to the family members to whom you have already spoken.

Q. Can a funeral service be held at a funeral home rather than at a church?
A. Yes, it can. This occurs most often when the deceased has not had a particular religious affiliation.

Q. I recently attended a funeral where I did not personally know the deceased but to show support for the family I do know. At the end of the funeral I wasn't sure if I should walk past the casket or not?
A. Even though you did not know the deceased it is a sign of respect to walk past the casket when your turn comes. It would seem uncaring for you not to do so.

Q. Does everyone wear black when attending a funeral?
A. No, it is no longer considered necessary to wear black unless you sit with the family or have been asked to be one of the honorary pallbearers. However, you should wear clothes that are subdued in color and inconspicuous. On no account should children be put into black at any time. They wear their best conservative clothes to a funeral.

Q. Does everyone who attends a funeral also attend the burial?
A. Only if the burial is in the churchyard or within walking distance of the church does the congregation follow the family to the graveside. Otherwise, those attending the funeral, wherever the services are held, do not go to the interment unless they are family members or close friends or unless the funeral director makes a general announcement about how cars will form a processional outside which indicates that anyone who wishes to continue on should do so.

Q. What is a memorial service? How does it differ from a funeral? Does a memorial service replace a funeral service?

A. A memorial service takes the place of a funeral, after the deceased has been buried or cremated privately or when the deceased has died in another country or perhaps in an airplane accident or accident at sea. If it takes place very shortly after the death, the service is very much like a funeral service. If it takes place much later, however, it is more often very brief. In general outline: Two verses of a hymn are sung, short prayers follow, and a very brief address is given about the work and life of the one for whom the service is held. It is closed with a prayer and a verse or two of another hymn.

Usually no flowers are sent except those for the altar.

An alternative to a memorial service is a "Service of Thanksgiving for the Life of (John Doe)." The service is simple, consisting of two or three tributes or eulogies given by friends or relatives, a prayer by the clergyman or clergywoman, and perhaps two or three hymns or musical offerings that were favorites of the deceased.

Q. Is it proper to have a receiving line after a memorial service?

A. Yes, it is. Since there generally are no formal visiting hours at a funeral home when a memorial service rather than an immediate funeral is held, a receiving line affords those who attend the service the chance to express their sympathy to family members.

Q. What is the purpose of a reception after a memorial service or funeral? Those I have attended have seemed like parties and I think this is inappropriate. Do you agree?
A. As long as the reception does not turn into a raucous affair, I see nothing wrong with this practice. It serves the purpose of giving friends and family the opportunity to gather, share their memories, and give support and love to one another.

Q. Where should a reception after a funeral or memorial service be held?
A. A reception may be held in the hall of the church. If this is the case, the minister should be asked to invite all present to the hall following the service. Generally, coffee and cakes are served and, if a formal receiving line is not held at the back of the church, it may be formed in the hall so that mourners may speak to each family member.

A reception may also be held in the home of the spouse or children of the deceased, or at the home of a close friend or other family member. If the host has the space and wishes to extend an invitation to all present, again the minister would announce this during the service. If space is limited and the reception is for only some of the guests, then one of the family members in the receiving line would say, "Please come back to the house with us, afterward."

In this case, either a caterer or friend has

remained at the host house to prepare for guests. Usually an informal buffet is provided, along with beverages.

Q. *How does a family acknowledge expressions of sympathy?*
A. Flowers, messages, Mass cards, personal condolences, contributions, and special kindnesses must all be acknowledged. Printed condolence cards with no personal message added and calls at the funeral home need not be acknowledged.

A personal message on a fold-over card is the preferable form for acknowledging expressions of sympathy. The note may be brief, but should be warm and mention the specific kindness or floral arrangement, etc. Printed or engraved cards may also be used, as long as a personal handwritten note is added below the printed message. If the condolences have come from strangers, however, as is often the case when a public figure or a member of his family dies and hundreds of impersonal messages are received, an engraved or printed card need not include a handwritten addition. Printed cards usually read:

> *The family of*
> *Harrison L. Winthrop*
> *wishes to thank you for*
> *your kind expression of sympathy*

If the list of personal acknowledgments to be sent is very long, or if the person who has received the flowers and messages is really unable to perform the task of writing, a member of the family or a near friend may write for him or her: "Mother asks me to thank you for your beautiful flowers and kind message of sympathy."

Letters must also be written to honorary pallbearers and ushers, thanking them for their service and perhaps noting how much their presence meant to the family.

Q. *Several months ago my 87-year-old grandfather died. When people heard the news and told us "I'm sorry" we were unsure how to respond. "Thank you" didn't seem right. What would be the appropriate response?*
A. There are several ways of responding to "I'm sorry." You might say, "Yes, we are going to miss him so much," or "I really appreciate your sympathy," or "Yes, he was a wonderful person, wasn't he?"

Q. *Who should attend a funeral of a business associate?*
A. If the funeral is not private, anyone who worked closely with the deceased should attend the funeral, even though he or she may not know any of the family members.

Invitations and Replies

Q. *What occasions call for formal third-person invitations? How is the invitation worded?*
A. The rule of thumb is that formal events require formal invitations. Occasions could include weddings, balls, formal dinner parties, dances, receptions, teas, commencements, bar and bat mitzvahs, and other official, state, or diplomatic parties.

  The invitation is worded in the third person. For example:

> *Mr. and Mrs. Robert Werner*
> *request the pleasure of your company*
> *at dinner*
> *on Saturday, the fourth of July*
> *at half past seven o'clock*
> *Seabreeze*
> *Edgartown, Massachusetts*
>
> *R.s.v.p.*
> *Box 636*
> *Edgartown, Massachusetts 02539*

Punctuation is used only when words requiring separation occur on the same line, and in certain abbreviations, such as "R.s.v.p." The time should never be given as "nine-thirty," but as "half past nine o'clock," or the more conservative form, "half after nine o'clock."

If the dance or dinner or other entertainment is to be given at one address and the hostess lives at another, both addresses are always given, assuming that the hostess wishes replies to go to her home address.

Q. How far in advance of an occasion are invitations sent out?
A. Depending on the type of occasion it is, invitations are usually sent between four and six weeks ahead of time, and should be answered at once. If a party is held at a catering hall or restaurant the caterer often wants to know the number of guests attending at least two weeks before the party, so prompt replies are essential. Wedding invitations are often sent up to six weeks ahead also, for this reason.

Q. How is the reply to a formal invitation worded when . . .
. . . you are accepting the invitation?
A. The general rule is "reply-in-kind." The formal reply is written exactly as is the invitation, substituting the order of names. In accepting the invitation you must repeat the day and hour so that any mistake can be rectified. But if you decline an invitation it is not necessary to repeat the hour.

If the invitation reads:

> *Mr. and Mrs. George de Menocal*
> *request the pleasure of your company*
> *at dinner*
> *on Saturday, the ninth of September*
> *at half past seven o'clock*
> *1411 Kenwood Parkway*
> *Miami Beach, Florida 33140*

R.s.v.p.

the acceptance reply would read:

> *Mr. and Mrs. Frank Kemp*
> *accept with pleasure*
> *the kind invitation of*
> *Mr. and Mrs. George de Menocal*
> *for dinner*
> *on Saturday, the ninth of September*
> *at half past seven o'clock*

Q. . . . *you must decline the invitation?*
A.

> *Mr. and Mrs. Scott Dunn*
> *regret that they are unable to accept*
> *the kind invitation of*
> *Mr. and Mrs. George de Menocal*
> *for Saturday, the ninth of September*

Q. *How is a wedding invitation worded?*
A. The following wording is correct for weddings of any size:

> *Mr. and Mrs. Hunter Wilson*
> *request the honour of your presence*
> *at the marriage of their daughter*
> *Catherine Elizabeth*
> *to*
> *Mr. Todd Campbell*
> *Saturday, the fifth of April*
> *half after four o'clock*
> *Church of St. John the Divine*
> *Minneapolis*

Q. *How are less formal invitations worded? How is the response worded?*
A. Less formal invitations may be a note, handwritten on an informal card:

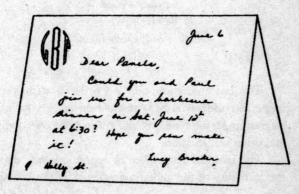

or they may be purchased, fill-in invitations:

> ### you are invited by
>
> **for**
> **on**   **at**   **o'clock**
> **at**

or they may be printed with the printed lines following the wording of the formal, third-person invitation:

> *Mr. and Mrs. Arnold Davidson*
> *request the pleasure of*
> *Dr. and Mrs. Reid Coleman's*
> *company at dinner*
> *on Saturday, the second of March*
> *at eight o'clock*
> *44 High Street*
> *Columbus, Ohio 43200*
>
> *R.s.v.p.*

The last invitation may be ordered with your name and address already printed on it, or you may buy an unpersonalized set and fill in your own name and other information.

The form of acceptance or regret depends upon the formality of the invitation received. If the R.s.v.p.

information is a telephone number, then your response is made by telephone, if possible. If you are unable to reach the host by telephone a note is always acceptable as long as it is prompt and there is time for it to be received well in advance of the day of the event. If the R.s.v.p. information is an address, a hand-written reply on your own informal or following the form of the printed, fill-in invitation is expected.

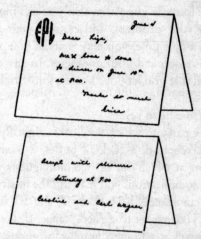

Q. Is it acceptable to extend invitations by telephone?
A. Yes. Telephone invitations are correct for all but the most formal dinners.

Q. I've been invited to a cocktail buffet which is being held the weekend my cousin is visiting. May I ask my hostess if my cousin may attend?
A. No. When regretting an invitation because you have a guest yourself, you should explain your reason

to the hostess. She then has the option to say, "I'm sorry you can't come—we'll miss you!" or, if she feels the addition of your cousin won't make a difference in her planning, she may say, "Do bring him. I'd love to meet your cousin."

Q. Can I change my response to an invitation . . .
. . . from yes to no?
A. Yes, but it is important that you call immediately, explain your problem, and express your regrets. If there is ample time, you may write, if you prefer, giving the reason and your apologies. In any event, it is essential that you let your hostess know right away.

Q. . . . from no to yes?
A. If the party to which you were originally invited is a large reception, a cocktail buffet, a picnic, or any gathering at which one or two more guests would not cause a complication, you may call the hostess, explain that circumstances have changed, and ask if you may change your regret to an acceptance. If, however, the party involves a limited number of guests, such as a seated dinner, a theater party, or bridge, the hostess will surely have filled your place and it would embarrass her if you asked to be reinstated.

Q. What is a response card and how is it used?
A. A response card, or answer card, is the least preferable form of obtaining a reply to an invitation, but it is acceptable. It is usually a small card that is engraved in the same style as the invitation it accompanies.

Response cards have a place for the invited guest to check whether he or she will attend or not. It is not a good idea to have a fill-in space for "number that will attend" since some recipients assume this means they may bring additional guests. Answer cards with invitations to private parties usually include a self-addressed, stamped envelope.

---

mr. Warren Harris

☐ **accepts**

☐ **regrets**

Friday, January second
Columbus Country Club

Q. I received a wedding invitation which included a response card. I am unable to attend the wedding. May I write a note explaining my regret at not being able to attend rather than return the response card?
A. You should use the card for your reply. The sender has undoubtedly organized a system for filing the returned cards, and a handwritten answer on notepaper would not fit in with the cards. You may, however, accompany the card with a handwritten note explaining your regret, so long as it is included with the card, not in lieu of the card.

Q. How soon after receiving an invitation should the guests respond?
A. As soon as they know if they can accept or must regret the invitation.

Q. If an invitation is addressed to Mr. and Mrs. does it include their children?
A. No, it does not. Only if the invitation was addressed "Mr. and Mrs. and family" or "and children" or if it listed the children's names after the adults' names are the children included in the invitation.

Q. May an unmarried person bring a guest to a wedding?
A. Of course, if his or her invitation reads "and guest." If it does not, then the invitation is intended only for the person to whom it is addressed.

Q. When I receive a wedding invitation addressed to me "and guest" do I tell the bride and groom my guest's name when I respond?
A. Yes, you should give her the name and address of your friend. Although it is not absolutely necessary, she may, at this time, send your guest an invitation. Even if she chooses not to, it is helpful to have your guest's name to prepare a place card for the reception if it's a seated dinner.

Q. How does a wedding announcement differ from an invitation?
A. Announcements are just that—they announce that

a wedding has taken place and they are sent after the wedding.

Q. *How is a wedding announcement worded? When are they sent? Who usually receives wedding announcements?*
A. It is never mandatory to send wedding announcements, but they are useful as a means of informing old friends who have been out of touch, business clients, people who live too far away to be able to attend, and closer friends who cannot be included when the wedding and reception lists are small. Announcements are never sent to anyone who has received an invitation to the ceremony and/or the reception. Announcements are sent as soon after the wedding as possible, preferably the next day. If there is an extenuating circumstance they may, however, be mailed up to several months later.

A wedding announcement may be worded as follows:

Mr. and Mrs. James Welch
have the honour of
announcing the marriage of their daughter
Christine Nicole
to
Mr. Thomas Charles Anders
Saturday, the twenty-seventh of March
One thousand nine hundred and ninety-seven
Washington, D.C.

I feel, however, that it is especially nice if the family of the groom is included on the announcement with that of the bride, even though the bride's family pays for the announcements. This indicates an attitude of joining and the approval and joy the groom's family feels in the marriage:

Mr. and Mrs. Winthrop Hastings
and
Mr. and Mrs. William Kienzle
announce the marriage of
Erin Kristin Hastings
and
Kenneth Burns Kienzle
Saturday, the twenty-seventh of March
Nineteen hundred and ninety-six
Trinity Church
New Milford, Connecticut

Q. *What obligation does a wedding announcement carry?*
A. None. As with an invitation to the wedding ceremony only, the receipt of an announcement does not demand a gift in return. Of course a gift may be sent, but it is not expected.

Celebrations

Q. *Who is invited to an engagement party? Are gifts brought to and opened at an engagement party?*
A. The guest list is unlimited, but the majority of engagement parties are restricted to relatives and good friends.

Engagement gifts are not expected from ordinary friends and acquaintances. They usually are given only by relatives and very special friends, and they generally are given to the bride alone. Sometimes they are given by the groom's family as a special welcome to the bride. Unless the custom in your family or your area is to bring gifts to the engagement party, in which case they are opened as part of the party, they should not be given at that time. It can cause embarrassment to those who have not brought anything. If guests do bring gifts, the bride should open them in private with only the donor present rather than making a display of them in front of those who did not bring anything.

Q. *How would a newspaper announcement of an engagement be worded?*
A. Each newspaper has its own special wording, and

many have forms for you to complete from which they write the announcement themselves. Send your announcement to the society editor one to two weeks before it is to run. The date on which you would like the news to be published should be given to all papers so that the notices will appear simultaneously. The usual form for the announcement is as follows:

> Mr. and Mrs. Jacob Graham of Albany, New York, announce the engagement of their daughter, Frances [Mary Graham—*optional*], to Mr. Eugene Weiss, son of Mr. and Mrs. Donald William Weiss of East Lansing, Michigan. A May wedding is planned.
>
> Miss Graham was graduated from The State University of New York at Albany and is now Director of Special Education in Albany. Mr. Weiss was graduated from Michigan State University. He is at present associated with Highland Hotels in Albany.

Q. Are engraved engagement announcements in good taste?
A. No. You may, and should, however, send notes to or call relatives and close friends to inform them of your engagement before an engagement party or newspaper announcement. This prevents them from reading it first in the newspapers and consequently suffering hurt feelings.

Q. Is there a set rule on who should and should not

have bridal or baby showers for family members?
A. The only people who are not "eligible" to give showers are immediate family. That generally means mothers, mothers-in-law, and sisters. Aunts, nieces, and cousins are not immediate family and may host a shower.

Q. *How do guests dress for . . .*
. . . a formal daytime wedding?
A. Women guests should wear street-length afternoon or cocktail dresses. Colors are preferable to all black or all white.

Men should wear dark suits, conservative shirts, and ties.

Q. *. . . a formal evening wedding?*
A. Women guests, depending on local custom, should wear long or short dresses. Head coverings and gloves are optional.

If women wear long dresses, men should wear tuxedos. If women wear short dresses, men may wear tuxedos or dark suits.

Q. *. . . a semiformal daytime wedding?*
A. Women guests wear short afternoon or cocktail dresses.

Men should wear dark suits, conservative shirts, and a tie.

Q. *. . . a semiformal evening wedding?*
A. Women guests may wear cocktail dresses.

Men guests wear dark suits, conservative shirts, and a tie.

Q. . . . an informal daytime wedding?
A. Women guests wear afternoon dresses. A head covering for church is optional.

Men guests wear dark suits or light trousers and dark blazers in summer.

Q. . . . an informal evening wedding?
A. Women guests wear afternoon or cocktail dresses.

Men guests wear dark suits, conservative shirts, and a tie.

Q. How can a bride make it known she'll be using her own name after the wedding? Can she include a small card with the invitation?
A. An addition to the end of the wedding announcement for the newspaper reading, "Miss Harris plans to retain her maiden name," is a good way to make it known. A card included with the invitation is not appropriate, but "at home" cards included with announcements sent after the wedding clearly impart the information:

Marissa Cartozian
and
Timothy Greeley
at home after the third of November
[etc.]

Q. *We are having our first baby soon and want to send birth announcements but are fearful people will think they are a bid for gifts. Do birth announcements obligate the receivers to send a gift?*

A. No. Birth announcements carry no obligation. They do not mean that the recipients need send gifts. It is thoughtful, however, for those who receive announcements to send a note of congratulations to the new parents.

Q. *Is there a standard form for birth announcement cards? Are birth announcements sent to local newspapers? If so, how would one be worded?*

A. No, there is no standard form. There is a large variety of commercially designed announcement cards available, as well as a large selection of announcements available through printers. Often parents design their own announcements, which can be the nicest cards of all. One of the nicest types of birth announcements, and the most traditional, consists of a very small card with space for the baby's name and birth date on it, tied with a pink or blue ribbon to the top of the "Mr. and Mrs." card of the parents.

Cori Cohen

March 14, 1995

Dr. and Mrs. Kenneth H. Cohen

39 Flagstaff Drive
Tucson, Arizona

Birth announcements may be sent to newspapers in the week following the birth: "Mr. and Mrs. Steven Krieger of 1009 Chesterfield Parkway, Columbus, announce the birth of a son, Benjamin, on July 2, 1995, at Doctor's Hospital. They have one daughter, Beth, three. Mrs. Krieger is the former Miss Barbara Dillon."

Q. May we send birth announcements when we adopt a child?
A. Most certainly. An announcement for an adopted child will bring reassuring comfort to the child later on, should he or she ever doubt his place in the hearts of the family who chose him.

> *Mr. and Mrs. Jason Black*
> *have the happiness to announce*
> *the adoption of*
> *Courtney*
> *age four months*

Or if announcements are sent during the legal proceedings, the wording may be changed:

> *Mr. and Mrs. Michael Newgaard*
> *have the happiness to announce*
> *the arrival of*
> *Sarah*
> *June twelfth, 1995*
> *age one month*

If you choose to use a commercial birth announcement for your adopted child, choose one in which you can easily insert the words *adopted* or *adoption* and one appropriate to the child's age. In other words, don't select a card with a picture of a stork with a baby in its mouth to announce the arrival of a two-year-old. If you prefer to design your own card, one of the nicest I've seen was the card sent by a family who already had a son and a daughter:

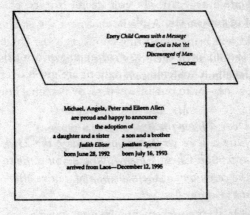

*Every Child Comes with a Message
That God is Not Yet
Discouraged of Man
—TAGORE*

Michael, Angela, Peter and Eileen Allen
are proud and happy to announce
the adoption of

a daughter and a sister   a son and a brother
Judith Ellisor   *Jonathan Spencer*
born June 28, 1992   born July 16, 1993

arrived from Laos—December 12, 1996

Q. *Is it proper to have a shower for a friend who has adopted a baby?*
A. Of course it is! A shower for a new baby, up to one year old, is a wonderful welcome and affirmation of a newly formed family.

Q. *I have recently received invitations to baby showers for third and fourth children in a family. I am on a*

fixed income, and while I am very happy for these families, I really can't afford to participate in ongoing celebrations that require gifts. Have you any advice?
A. A baby shower held for a first or even second child is fine, but it becomes an imposition to ask the same people to a third or fourth baby shower. However, you are not obligated to accept these invitations nor to send a gift if you do not go. Simply refuse politely, and send the prospective or new parents a congratulatory card. If you decide to accept, you must of course, take a gift.

Q. *How are invitations to a christening or brit issued?*
A. Usually, christening invitations are given over the telephone—or to out-of-towners, by personal note:

> *Dear Annemarie and George,*
> *Julie will be christened on Sunday, the 23rd, at 3:00 in Christ Church. Would you come to the ceremony at the church, and join us afterward at our house?*
>
> > *Love,*
> > *Allison*

Or a message may be written on the "Mr. and Mrs." cards of the parents or on an informal card, saying simply, "Julie's christening, Christ Church, March 23rd, 3 o'clock. Reception at our house afterward." All invitations to a christening should be very friendly and informal.

For a *brit*, relatives and close friends are invited by telephone since the time between birth and the ceremony is short.

Q. *How should godparents be chosen?*
A. One must never ask any but a most intimate friend or relative to be a godparent, for it is a responsibility not to be undertaken lightly and also one difficult to refuse.

Q. *What are the obligations of a godparent toward their godchild?*
A. The obligation of being a godparent is essentially a spiritual one which recommends that the godparent be of the same faith as the parents. The godparent vows to see that the child is given religious training, learns the specific creeds and commandments of the church, and is confirmed at the proper time.

Beyond these obligations he is expected to take a special interest in the child, much as a very close relative would do, remembering him or her with a gift on birthdays and on Christmas until the child is grown—or perhaps longer if they remain close.

Godparents who have lost contact with the child and his or her parents need not continue to give presents after the threads of friendship have broken.

Godparents do not have any obligation to give financial assistance or to assume the care of children who lose their parents. This responsibility is the guardian's—not the godparent's.

Q. *Who provides the christening outfit, the parents or the godparents?*
A. The parents do. The dress may be new, or is often one that was worn by the baby's mother, father, or even one of his or her grandparents or great-grandparents. Usually everything the baby wears is white, although this is a custom, not a church requirement.

Q. *Who hosts an anniversary party? May the couple host the party or do family members plan the party?*
A. Early anniversary parties are always given by the couple themselves. By the time they reach the twenty-fifth they may well have grown children who wish to make the arrangements, but it is perfectly correct for them to do so themselves if the young people do not or cannot. When a couple do not have children, close friends sometimes prepare the celebration. Fiftieth-anniversary celebrations are almost invariably planned by the family of the couple.

Q. *What type of invitation is appropriate for an anniversary party?*
A. The form of the invitations depends entirely on the degree of formality of the party. They may range from an informal telephone call to an engraved third-person invitation. Formal invitations for a twenty-fifth anniversary are often bordered and printed in silver; those for a fiftieth, in gold. The most common forms are handwritten notes, or the necessary information written on an informal or a fill-in card.

Q. *My husband and I are planning to reaffirm our wedding vows for our tenth anniversary. The service and reception will be held at our home with about 100 guests. We would prefer no gifts to us personally. Instead we would like to enclose a separate card in the invitation stating that the traditional gift of ten years is tin/aluminum and that a basket will be provided for donations of canned goods to an organization that feeds the hungry. We don't know how to word the card without sounding like we assumed people were planning on giving us gifts. We want to tie traditional ideas with a modern need without offending would-be guests. Can you help?*

A. You can be sure that people would expect to bring you a gift on your tenth anniversary, so don't worry about that. Enclose a card, or write on the invitation, "In lieu of a 10th anniversary gift of tin or aluminum, we invite you to contribute to a basket of canned food to be sent to World Hunger Relief " (or "to our local food pantry for the homeless and hungry"). There would be less hunger in the world if there were more people like you!

Q. *When graduation draws near, I will be very proud to send graduation announcements to relatives, but how do I know which of my friends, my parents' friends, or friends of the family to send announcements to without making it look like I am showing off or expecting a gift? Do I send to other graduating friends in other schools? Do I send to friends of the family or my parents' friends whose children have*

never sent graduation announcements to my family?
A. Graduation announcements should only be sent to relatives and close friends. They are not usually sent to friends graduating from other schools or to children of your parents' friends.

Q. *My son is a senior in high school and will be graduating in the spring. I would like to send graduation announcements to a few select friends and relatives without them thinking they must send money or a gift. Would it be appropriate to include a note "no gifts"?*
A. Announcements do not carry any obligation, but many people do not know that and feel they must send a gift. Either send the announcements to very close friends and relatives who would want and expect to send a gift, or have "no gifts please" written on the announcements if you are adamant about this point.

Q. *Is it incorrect to give our own housewarming party?*
A. No, it is a very nice thing to do. When you have put a great deal of time and effort into making a lovely home you are naturally as eager to show it off as your friends are to see it. A housewarming is generally a cocktail party or a cocktail buffet. It may be as simple or as elaborate as you wish.

Q. *Some very close friends are moving away and I would like to have a farewell party for them. Is this appropriate? Do people bring gifts?*
A. It is perfectly appropriate. It is a good idea to

coordinate your plans with other friends so that the guests of honor are not exhausted by several farewell parties. I know a popular couple who moved away from my hometown recently, and there were thirteen parties held for them! By the time the departure date arrived, their exhausted friends could hardly wait for them to go! Friends are expected to take farewell gifts to a party, but if there is one particular gift that would be too expensive for individuals to give, you could coordinate its purchase, requesting a reasonable contribution from the guests who are able to attend. This should be noted on the invitation—"We will be giving John and Mary a watercolor of their house here, as a memory from all of us. A contribution of $10 to Jean Gould, 10 Adams Street, would be appreciated. Your name will be signed on the card that will accompany the gift." This indicates that the gift is taken care of, and delegating the collection toward it to another friend frees the hostess to plan the party.

Q. Should I give a retirement party for my father, for our family and friends to attend?
A. Retirement parties are usually given by professional associates, but relatives or close friends may certainly give a party too.

Q. Suddenly, birthday parties for adult friends are being given. Is this socially correct?
A. Certainly! There is no limit on the kind of celebration this may be, from a barbecue or picnic to a formal dinner dance at a club or restaurant. The only real

requirement is that at some point during the party, the host or hostess asks for the attention of the assembled guests and offers a toast to the birthday person. Often guests wish to make their own toasts, read a poem or verse prepared especially for the guest of honor, or make a speech about the birthday person. Invitations may be preprinted, fill-in, or even telephone calls, depending on the formality of the event. Because it is a birthday party, it is assumed that gifts are to be taken, unless the invitation indicates "no gifts please." The guest of honor may elect to open the gifts during or after the party, depending on its formality and other activities occurring during the party.

On the subject of gifts, it should be said that the most frequent awkwardness about gift-giving to an adult at his or her birthday party has to do with the type of gift to give—a "real" gift, or a "gag" gift. It can be embarrassing when gifts are opened and yours is the only "over the hill" present among luxury items given by everyone else. If you are not certain which direction to take, call the host and ask. If the host replies, "Oh, don't bring a gift!" rather than, "Yes, people are bringing nice presents, not gag gifts," ask if you may have the names of one or two others invited to the party so that you can check with them also.

Q. *Do you think that children should open birthday gifts at their birthday parties?*
A. Yes, I do. I know that some parents don't trust that their child won't say, "I already have this!" or "I

hate this present," not meaning to be insensitive, but because they are basically honest and blunt. Other parents don't want the guests at the party taking gifts and using them before the birthday child has a chance to play with them. Both these situations are readily resolved, and provide an important opportunity for a child, who has likely participated in the gift selection for other friends, to see his gift opened.

Parents should help a child prepare for what to say when a duplicate gift is received, or when they open something they don't like or can't use. For example, I know a fifteen-year-old girl who has not pierced her ears, and probably never will. Her friends continue to give her pierced earrings for her birthday. She graciously exclaims over them, and says how much she will look forward to wearing them as soon as she gets her ears pierced. She is very reassuring to the donors, who are embarrassed that they didn't notice that her ears weren't pierced, telling them that she will be so lucky to have such pretty earrings to start her collection. In the same way, a small child can be told that it might hurt a friend's feelings to announce that he already has something he receives as a gift, or that if he receives the same game or toy from two friends he can say how great it is because that means more people can play with them at the same time. He should be told that it is important to exclaim, "Thank you!" when he opens a gift, even if he doesn't like it.

When children are small and want immediately to play with gifts as they are opened, it is important for an adult to set gifts aside, after they have been admired, with a comment that Becky may want a chance to look at all her presents again before they are used by anybody else.

Q. *Do you have any advice for a way to keep children at a large party from all crowding around the birthday child as she opens her gifts?*
A. A very nice way to handle this is to place the birthday child in a large chair and have each guest present his gift and sit next to the birthday child as the card is read and the gift is opened. This gives special attention to each guest, and lets all the children know that they will have a turn to be close to the birthday child. Make it clear that the guest returns to the circle after his present is opened, to make room for the next person.

Gifts and Thank-yous

Q. When is it acceptable to give money as a gift?
A. In most cases a gift other than money is the proper choice, but there are some exceptions. Many ethnic groups traditionally give money as a wedding gift, and often money is given for a religious confirmation, a first communion, a bar or bat mitzvah, and a graduation. Another occasion for which a gift of money is not inappropriate is a fiftieth anniversary. Many older couples, perhaps living on a pension or Social Security, appreciate cash more than gifts, which they neither need nor have room for.

For people who dislike the idea of giving a check or cash, a gift certificate is a good compromise.

Q. We have received invitations to birthday and anniversary parties that state "No Gifts Please." Does this also include money gifts? I never know what to do.
A. When an invitation says "no gifts please," it means just that—*no* gifts, money or otherwise, should be brought to the party. It is only embarrassing to the host and to those who do not bring gifts if some guests ignore the request. When someone does ignore this sincere request, the gift he brings should not be

opened during the party or put on display. It should be opened at a later time, in private, and the donor thanked by note.

If it is your tradition to exchange gifts on these occasions you may drop it off or have it delivered to their home before or after the party.

Q. Should gifts be opened at a party?
A. Yes. Half the fun of giving and receiving presents at any party is to see and enjoy what everyone else brought. The nicest way to do this is to have all the presents collected in one place until everyone has arrived, at which time the guest of honor opens them. The recipient reads the cards enclosed and shows enthusiasm for each gift, no matter how peculiar some may be. If anyone has given money instead of a present, the amount should not be mentioned but the recipient may well say something like, "This is a really welcome contribution toward the china we are saving for," or whatever else may be appropriate.

On occasions when gifts are not necessarily expected, but two or three people bring them regardless, they are opened in the donor's presence but without drawing the attention of the other guests. This might happen, for instance, when a couple brings a gift to a dinner hostess. She must show her appreciation, but making a display of the present could embarrass guests who did not bring one.

Q. How can you respond when someone arrives with an unexpected gift at Christmastime?

A. Unless you have a supply of small gifts or tins of home-baked goods ready for such an emergency you can only say, "Thanks so much—but you shouldn't have done this," to indicate that you do not expect to start an annual exchange of gifts.

Q. Which is better—to send flowers to your hosts before or after a party?
A. When a party is given especially for you, you should send flowers to your hostess beforehand. Otherwise, flowers sent later as a thank-you for a very special evening are always appreciated.

Q. Should guests bring gifts of food or wine to their hosts?
A. The custom of taking wine as a gift to a small dinner party is becoming customary. It is not too expensive or elaborate and has the advantage that if the hostess does not want to serve it that evening because she has planned another type of wine or a different beverage, she need not do so. She certainly may offer it, but no guest should feel insulted if his hostess says, "Thanks so much! I already have wine planned for dinner, but we'll look forward to enjoying this another time!"

Gifts of food to be used for the dinner should never be given unless the hostess has been consulted first. It is very disconcerting for a hostess who has planned a dessert to complement her meal to feel she must also serve another, unexpected dessert which may be too rich or uncomplementary. A box of candy, croissants, and jam for the hosts' breakfast the next morning, or another gift of food given with the statement, "This is for you to enjoy tomorrow," resolves the problem.

If it is the custom in your area to take a gift to a small dinner party, by all means do so. For a large or formal party, however, it is better not to take a gift at all, especially if you do not know the hosts well. It may not be customary among their friends, and you will only embarrass your hostess and other guests who have not brought a gift. If you do know the hosts well and you have noticed that people generally do arrive with a gift, then follow the custom of the area.

Q. *What gifts are returned when an engagement is broken? What about wedding gifts if the marriage lasts only a short time?*
A. All gifts except those that are monogrammed should be returned if an engagement is broken, including the engagement ring and any gifts of value received from a fiancé or fiancée. Shower gifts, too, should be returned if the marriage is called off. Once the wedding has taken place, however, gifts are not returned, no matter how short-lived the marriage, unless the wedding is annulled before the couple lives together.

Q. *What do I do if a gift arrives broken?*
A. If it arrives directly from a local store, take it with its wrappings to the shop where it was purchased. If it comes from another city or a mail-order

company, return it by mail, accompanied by a letter explaining how it arrived. Any good store or company will replace the merchandise on reasonable evidence that it was received in a damaged condition. Do not involve the donor in this or even let him or her know what happened if you can possibly avoid doing so.

If the package was packed and mailed by the donor, not a store, and it was insured, you must let the sender know so he or she can collect the insurance and replace the gift. If the package was not insured, it is best not to mention the damaged condition since the sender will feel obligated to replace the gift at his own, duplicate expense.

Q. May duplicate wedding gifts be exchanged? Do I tell the donor?

A. Yes, duplicate wedding gifts may be exchanged, so long as they are not from the bride or bridegroom's family. If they suggest that the bride exchange the gift for something else naturally she may do so.

When a duplicate gift is received from someone who lives far away and is not likely to visit the bride and groom soon, the couple need not mention the fact that they are exchanging a present on their thank-you note. However, it would be wise to explain the exchange to someone who will be in their house and will surely notice the absence of the gift. If you do mention the exchange to the donor, it is important to mention in your thank-you note that you are enjoying what you got as a replacement, thanks to them.

Q. Are wedding presents addressed to the bride alone, or to both the bride and groom?

A. A wedding present given before the wedding is addressed to the bride alone. A gift given after the wedding is addressed to both the bride and the groom.

Q. When and where are wedding gifts delivered? Are gifts brought to a wedding reception?

A. Gifts are generally delivered to the bride's home before the day of the wedding. They may be delivered in person or they may be sent directly from the store where they were purchased.

In some localities and among certain ethnic groups it is customary to take your gift to the wedding reception rather than send it ahead of time. Checks are usually handed to the bride and groom as you go through the receiving line, but gift packages are placed on a table prepared for them, as soon as you arrive. If there is a large number of presents, the bride and groom do not open them until a later date, so that they will have time to enjoy the other festivities. If there are only a few, however, they should open them after the receiving line breaks up. One of the bride's attendants should help, disposing of wrappings and keeping a careful list of the gifts.

Q. I would love to have a bridal shower for my friend who is marrying for the first time at age 60. She and her husband-to-be have fully furnished homes. I am at a loss for a theme. Any suggestions?

A. If there is literally nothing this couple needs (don't forget things like tickets to concerts or other entertainments, gift certificates to restaurants, or books as ideas), you could suggest that everyone make a donation to the bride's and groom's favorite charity. Their thank-you notes, then, would be based on notification received from the charity that such gifts had been given. So that they would have something to open at the shower, you could also ask guests to come with envelopes containing a handwritten note stating, "A contribution has been made to XYZ Association, in your name."

Q. Should gifts such as a baptism cup or a picture frame be monogrammed, or should I not have them marked in case the person I am giving them to doesn't like them?
A. The obvious drawback to monogramming a gift is that once an article has been initialed it can never be returned. Before you have anything of value marked, be sure it is something you know is wanted and also, in the case of clothing, that it is the right size, color, and style. If you are sure of this, then initials are a handsome addition to many gifts.

It is always possible for the receiver to have the gift marked later. If free engraving is offered with the purchase, it will be honored at any time later. If there is a charge, however, you should have the bill for the marking sent to you, and be sure that the recipient knows this. Better yet, if the recipient is pleased with the gift, it is thoughtful to take it back, have it marked yourself, and then return it.

Q. How soon after receiving a gift should the thank-you be written?
A. Thank-yous should be written promptly, particularly when a gift is received through the mail or United Parcel Service and the donor has no way of knowing if you received it or not. Although it is preferable that the bride and groom acknowledge all gifts as they are received, they may, if necessary, take up to three months, at the outside, to send their thank-yous.

Q. Under what circumstances are thank-you notes obligatory, optional, or unnecessary?
A. The most important qualifications of a thank-you letter are that it sound sincere and that it be written promptly. You use the expressions most natural to you and write as enthusiastically as you would speak. The chart on pages 156–159 tells you when thank-you notes are obligatory, optional, or unnecessary.

Q. What should I do when I don't receive any acknowledgment for a gift?
A. If you delivered the gift in person, you know it was received and that the recipient is exercising bad manners. If, however, you mailed the gift or had it sent from a store and have received no acknowledgment after three months at the outside, you must write and ask whether or not it was received.

It is inexcusable not to thank the donor for any

gift so if your letter embarrasses the recipient, that is fine. She or he should be embarrassed and perhaps will remember better manners in the future.

One suggestion is to send all gifts insured. You then have a good reason to write and say, "Since I haven't heard from you I assume the gift I sent was lost. If that is so I would like to put a claim in for the insurance, so would you let me know as soon as possible whether you received it or not."

When the gift in question is a check, you might write, "I am quite concerned about the check I sent you for your birthday. It has been cashed and returned to me, but since I have received no word from you I am worried that it fell into the wrong hands and it was not you who cashed it. Would you let me know?"

Q. Who writes the thank-you notes, the bride or the groom? How are they signed, with only the bride's or groom's name, or with both names?
A. Since most gifts are sent to the bride, she usually writes and signs the thank-you note, but there is no reason the groom should not share this task. There are many relatives and friends of the groom who would be delighted to receive a thank-you note from him.

It is not incorrect to sign both names, but it is preferable to sign only one name and include the other in the text: "Bob and I are so delighted with . . . , etc." or "Jean and I . . . , etc."

Thank-you Notes

Occasion	Obligatory
Dinner parties	Only if you are a guest of honor.
Overnight visits	Always, except in the case of close friends or relatives whom you see frequently. Then, a telephone call would serve the purpose.
For birthday, anniversary, Christmas, and other gifts	Always, when you have not thanked the donor in person. Here again, a phone call to a very close friend or relative is sufficient.
Shower gifts	If the donor was not at the shower or you did not extend verbal thanks.
Gifts to a sick person	Notes to out-of-towners and calls or notes to close friends are obligatory as soon as the patient feels well enough.
For notes of condolence	Thank-yous should be sent for all notes of condolence except for printed cards with no personal message.
For congratulatory cards or gifts	All personal messages must be acknowledged.

Optional or Unnecessary

Otherwise, always appreciated but not necessary if you have thanked your hostess when leaving.

It is never wrong to send a note in addition to your verbal thanks.

Many women like to add a written note to their verbal thanks, but it is not necessary.

Form letters from firms need not be acknowledged.

continued

Thank-you Notes *(cont.)*

Occasion	Obligatory
Wedding gifts	*Obligatory*—even though verbal thanks have been given. All wedding gifts must be acknowledged within three months, but preferably as the gifts arrive.
When a hostess receives a gift after visitors have left	Even though the gift is a thank-you itself, the hostess must thank her visitors, especially if the gift has arrived by mail, so that the visitor will know it has been received.
When a client is entertained by a sales representative	

Q. Are written thank-you notes necessary for gifts friends brought to the hospital when my baby was born?
A. No, if you give warm thanks at the time, you need not then write a note. However, when gifts are sent, a note—or a phone call, to close friends—is in order. The note may be written on an informal or on a thank-you card with a personal message. It should be signed with the mother's name, not the baby's.

Optional or Unnecessary

Even though the entertainment is charged to the sales representative's company it would not be remiss to send a note. It is not necessary, but might help to ensure a good relationship.

Tipping

Q. What guidelines can you give for tipping?
A. I believe firmly that a tip should be merited. Where service is bad and the personnel deliberately rude, inattentive, or careless, the amount should be reduced. If it is bad enough, no tip should be left at all, and you should bring the situation to the attention of the manager. On the other hand, rewarding good service more generously is just as important since most service people depend on tips to augment their usually low salary. Their effort to provide excellent service therefore should be appreciated.

For many years 15 percent has been the accepted percentage for a tip. As prices have increased some people wonder why the percentage has not increased also, but they fail to realize that 15 percent of a higher price results in a higher tip. Enough said.

With this as a basic guideline, the chart on the following pages gives general standards for tipping in most parts of the United States.

When Dining

An increasing number of restaurants in the United States are adding a service charge or gratuity to the bill. You should be aware of this and if it is the case where you are dining you need not pay any additional tip. This practice is more common when there are six or more in your party.

Recipient	Amount or Percentage to Tip
Bartender	15 to 20 percent of the bar bill if you have drinks at the bar before going to your table. It is given to him when he gives you your check or, if the bar bill is added to your dinner check, before you leave the bar.
Busboys	No tip except in cafeterias when busboy carries your tray to the table, in which case tip 50 cents.
Caterers	
at clubs or restaurants	If the service charge is added to the bill (usually 15 to 17 percent) the host is not obligated to do more unless he wishes to do so, except to the person in charge—headwaiter, maître d', or whoever it may be—who receives a separate tip of $5

When Dining (cont.)	
Recipient	**Amount or Percentage to Tip**
	to $10 or more, depending on the size and elaborateness of the party.
	If no service charge is added, the host gives the person in charge 15 to 20 percent of the bill and asks that he divide it among the waiters, plus $10 or more for the person in charge.
at home	Approximately 20 percent of the bill is given to be divided among the bartender, waiters and waitresses by the host before they leave, if gratuities are not to be included in the bill.
Checkroom attendant	Even if there is a charge for checking your coat, tip the attendant. When the charge is 75 cents per coat, tip 25 cents. If no charge, tip 50 cents per coat for more than one coat but $1 for one coat. No extra tip for parcels unless there are many.
Headwaiters	At a restaurant you patronize regularly, $5 to $10 from time to time.
	When he has done nothing but seat

When Dining *(cont.)*

Recipient	Amount or Percentage to Tip
	you and hand you a menu, no matter how many in your party, no tip.$5 or more if he arranges a special table, cooks a special dish in front of you, or offers other special services. Hand him your tip as you leave the restaurant.
Musicians	No tip to strolling player unless he plays specific request. Then the usual tip is $1. If several members of a large party make requests, up to $5. $1 to $2 to pianist or organist for playing your request.
Waiters and waitresses	15 to 18 percent of the bill, slightly higher for extraordinarily good service. 20 percent in very elegant restaurants. If hosting dinner party of ten, twelve, or more, 18 to 20 percent of bill is divided among the waiters and waitresses who serve you. Never less than 15 cents for cup of

When Dining (cont.)	
Recipient	Amount or Percentage to Tip
	coffee or soft drink only. Never less than 25 cents at lunch counter.
	In restaurant, tip left on tray on which check is brought or added to credit card.
	At lunch counter, tip left on counter.
Washroom attendants	Never less than 50 cents, sometimes $1 in expensive restaurant. Tip placed in dish or plate for that purpose. If attendant does nothing but sit and look at you, no tip necessary.
Wine steward	15 to 20 percent of wine bill when you are getting ready to leave. If wine charged to credit card separate from dinner order, tip may be added to charge slip at the time bill is presented.

While Traveling

Recipient	Amount or Percentage to Tip
Airplanes	Skycaps (porters) receive $1 a bag or $3 to $5 for a baggage cart full of luggage. (No tips ever for stewardesses, stewards, hostesses, or flight officers.)
Bus tours; charter buses	$5 to $10 on a long tour to both driver and guide, depending on length of tour, unless gratuities are included in the fare.
	No tip to charter and sightseeing bus drivers. Optional $1 to guides or driver-guides.
Cruise ships	
cabin and dining stewards	Check with travel agent, purser, or cruise director on the ship. Up to $5 per day or $25 per week, depending on which "class" you travel and the services you receive.
	or
	15 to 20 percent of total fare, with the larger proportion going to the

While Traveling *(cont.)*

Recipient	Amount or Percentage to Tip
	cabin steward and dining room steward. The remainder is divided between the head dining steward and the deck steward.
	Tip an appropriate proportion at end of each week so personnel has cash to spend during stops in ports.
lounge and bar stewards	15 to 20 percent of bill at time of service.
wine steward	15 percent of total wine bill.
bath steward	If no private bath, $1 when you reserve time for your bath.
cabin boy	At least 25 cents for each errand performed.
porter	$2 to $5 for heavy trunks, $1 per bag for suitcases.
cruise director	No tip ever.
ship's officers	No tip ever.

While Traveling *(cont.)*

Recipient	Amount or Percentage to Tip
when gratuities included in fare	$3 to $5 to someone who has been especially helpful.
Hotels and full-service motels (stays of one week or less)	
bellman or bellwoman	$1 per bag—more if very heavy—plus 50 cents for opening room.
	50 cents per bag plus 50 cents to $1 for opening room in smaller cities.
chambermaid	Take into account the size of your party and the amount of time you spend in the room. Adults who use the room to shower and sleep need not tip as much as a family where the parents go out to dinner each night and the children order room service.
	$5 to $10 a week per person in first-class hotel.
	$3 to $5 a week in small, inexpensive hotel.

While Traveling *(cont.)*

Recipient	Amount or Percentage to Tip
	No tip if staying only one night.
	Give tip in person if possible. If not, leave on bureau in envelope marked "chambermaid," or give to desk clerk and ask that he or she deliver it.
desk clerk	No tip unless special service is rendered, in which case $5 to $10 is ample.
dining room waiter	In first-class hotel restaurant, 18 to 20 percent of the bill.
door attendant	$1 per bag if he takes luggage into the hotel.
	No tip if he puts bag on sidewalk.
	$1 to $3 for calling a taxi or, if you are staying longer than a day or two, $5 at end of each week.
garage valet parking service	$2 in large cities and $1 in smaller cities each time car is delivered.
headwaiter	When you leave, tip in proportion to the services rendered: $3 to $5 a

While Traveling *(cont.)*

Recipient	Amount or Percentage to Tip
	week if he has done little, $10 a week if he has been especially attentive.
	No tip needed for one-night stay.
room waiter	15 percent of bill for each meal. This is in addition to hotel fee for room service.
valet	No tip.
Taxis	50 cents minimum for fare up to $2.50. For higher fares, tip 15 percent of meter.
	Same for unmetered cabs; pay 15 percent of fare.
Trains	
bar or club car waiters	15 to 20 percent of bill, as well as 50 cents for delivering setups to your sleeping car.
dining car waiters	15 to 20 percent of the bill and never less than 50 cents.
luggage porters	$1 in addition to fixed rate fee. If no

While Traveling *(cont.)*

Recipient	Amount or Percentage to Tip
	fixed rate fee, then $1 per bag.
sleeping car porter	At least $2 per person per night—more if he has given additional service other than making up berths.

At Health or Sports Clubs

Recipient	Amount or Percentage to Tip
Golf caddies	15 to 20 percent of the regular club charge for eighteen holes, closer to 20 percent for nine holes.
Instructors	No tip.
Locker-room attendant	$1 at time service rendered if he or she provides towels or other personal attention.
Masseur	20 percent of the cost of the massage.
Other personnel	Generally no tip at time of service. Often a members' collection at Christmastime for employees' fund.
	Give additional tips, usually $5 to $10, depending on type of club and

At Health or Sports Clubs *(cont.)*

Recipient	Amount or Percentage to Tip
	amount of service, to any employee who gives you personal attention— washroom attendant, locker-room attendants, headwaiter, etc.
	Sometimes additional tips for special services throughout year.
	Guests do not tip unless residents for a time, in which case, if no service charge added to bill, tip as you would in a first-class hotel.

Personal & Professional Services

Recipient	Amount or Percentage to Tip
Answering service	Minimum of $5 per operator who has a shift on your service, at Christmastime.
Au pair or live-in child care/ housekeeper	One week's extra salary at Christmastime, plus small gifts from children
Baby-sitters	For steady baby-sitters, double an average night's salary at Christ-

Personal & Professional Services

Recipient	Amount or Percentage to Tip
	mas—or a small gift from the children is thoughtful—in addition to tip at time of service, usually the equivalent of approximately one half to one hour's pay.
Barber	
for a child	In a rural area, 50 cents. In a city, $1 or 15 percent of bill is about average.
for an adult	Since the cost is higher than for a child, the tip should be correspondingly higher. $1 to $2 to the manicurist and for a shampoo, shave, etc., an equivalent amount depending on the type of shop and the number of services used. A regular customer does not tip the shop owner for each haircut, but gives him or her a gift at Christmas.
Beauty salon	15 percent to one stylist who shampoos, cuts, and sets or drys. 20 percent if several stylists divide services, as follows: 10 percent to the person who cuts, 10 percent

Personal & Professional Services *(cont.)*

Recipient	Amount or Percentage to Tip
	divided among the others.
	Generally no tip to a proprietor who cuts or sets your hair, although 10 percent is acceptable if you wish. If it is your first visit, watch what other customers do or ask the receptionist. Regular customers give a small gift at Christmas to the proprietor, stylist, and shampooer.
Butcher	If you receive regular deliveries one or more times a week, tip at least $5 per service deliverer at Christmastime.
Cleaner	If your dry cleaning is picked up and delivered regularly one or more times a week, tip at least $5 per service deliverer at Christmas.
Commercial messengers	If you use services on regular basis, $5 to $10 at Christmastime.
Dairy	If the dairy delivers regularly, one or more times a week, tip at least $5 per service deliverer at Christmastime.

Personal & Professional Services *(cont.)*

Recipient	Amount or Percentage to Tip
Diaper service	$5 at Christmastime or, if you keep the service for less than one year, when you terminate the service.
Florists	$1 to delivery person when you order flowers or floral arrangements sent to your home or when flowers are sent to you by someone else.
Garbage collectors	$5 to $10 per crew member at Christmastime for private service workers. Same to municipal workers if not in violation of local law.
Grocery loaders	50 cents to $1 for normal number of bags placed in car.
	$1 to $2 for large week's marketing.
Hospital staff	No money tips. It is proper to bring candy or the like that can be shared by all the staff caring for the patient. Give three of whatever the gift is, marked "1st shift," "2nd shift," "3rd shift." Otherwise the shift on duty at the time will enjoy it but seldom

Personal & Professional Services *(cont.)*

Recipient	Amount or Percentage to Tip
	leave any for the other shifts that have cared for the patient too.
private duty nurses	For prolonged duty, Christmas gift or gift on departing, but no money.
Hotels, residential	Permanent or long-term residents tip on monthly or even twice-yearly basis according to quality of service.

Household helpers

live-in help	$10 to $15 when extra work is required for large party.
	One week's pay at Christmastime.
part-time housecleaners	Approximately one week's pay at Christmastime.
when a guest in a private home	After weekend visit, $5 to host's maid and/or cook for a single guest, $10 for a couple.
	No tip ever to servants at a dinner party.

Personal & Professional Services *(cont.)*

Recipient	Amount or Percentage to Tip
Laundry service	If regular pick-up and delivery, at least $5 at Christmastime.
Letter carriers	According to the United States Postal Service, it is illegal to tip your letter carrier.
Movers and furniture deliverers	No tip for one or two crates or pieces of furniture. For larger loads or if movers perform special services (put furniture in place, lay carpets, etc.) at least $10 per person.
Newspaper carriers	$5 to $15 at Christmas, depending on number of days carrier delivers and the quality of service. 50 cents per week paid at time of regular collection.
Parking attendants	$1 to attendant who delivers car from garage in small cities; $1 to $2 in large cities.
	When you rent garage space monthly, attendants are not tipped for delivery but are given tips at Christmastime and occasionally throughout year for special services,

Personal & Professional Services *(cont.)*

Recipient	Amount or Percentage to Tip
	usually $5 each time.
Residential building employees at Christmas	Depending on size of building and staff and amount of services:
superintendent	$50 to $100 if he lives in, less if a janitor or other staff member does repairs.
door person	$35 to $50 to each doorman, plus occasional tips of $1 to $5 for special services, hailing taxicabs, accepting deliveries, etc.
janitor	Janitor or regular handyman, $10 to $20 depending on amount of service rendered.
elevator operators	$10 to $20.
Shoeshines	50 cents to $1 for shoes, $1 for boots at time service rendered.
Ushers	No tip at movie theater, concert hall, opera house, or theater.

Personal & Professional Services *(cont.)*

Recipient	Amount or Percentage to Tip
	$1 to $3 per party at an arena, for boxes and loges. No tip necessary in upper balconies and bleachers.

Q. Do I calculate my tip before or after the sales tax has been added?
A. It is permissible to calculate your tip on the amount of the bill before the tax. However, many people choose to figure the tip on the total amount of the bill, including the sales tax. Of course, as the price of meals increases the sales tax is correspondingly higher, a fact to keep in mind when you decide on the tip.

Q. I'm vacationing in Europe this year. Is tipping there done the same way as here at home?
A. No, generally it is a different system. In most European restaurants and hotels, a 15 to 18 percent (approximate) service charge is added to your bill. You are not expected to give additional tips. Do not tip the bellboy, maid, or concierge. Do not tip the waiters beyond service charge and if you wish, any small coins returned to you as change.

When no service charge is added to your bill, or if you think it is too low, tip exactly as you would in the United States.

Theater ushers are tipped in Europe, usually the equivalent of a quarter, but not in England. In England, there is generally a charge for the program instead.

Q. *Recently I had to buy a new refrigerator and then a new furnace. I also had new carpeting installed in my living room. I was very unsure as to whether I was supposed to tip the workmen who delivered and installed these items. Should I have done so?*

A. I often touch base with business managers in these areas to see what expectations and trends are. They tell me that a tip is never to be expected, but when given it is received with appreciation. The best rule of thumb is that service and installation personnel who are particularly thoughtful; who take care cleaning up after themselves; who take away with them old appliances, carpeting, or materials; and who deal with children, pets, and other intrusions on their work with kindness should probably be tipped. It goes slightly against the grain to tip people for doing their jobs, but this is exactly what we do when we tip the barber or the porter who carries our bags. Delivery persons and installers are indeed doing their jobs, but these days we often thank them with a tip for doing them well. The amount to be tipped depends on the amount of work done, but generally is $5-$10 per person for basic delivery and placement or installing.

When a job is complicated or the work intricate, such as the laying of carpeting on a stairway. the chief technician or installer can receive up to $20 and his or her assistant $5 to $10.

Be sure to check the bill before tipping, however.

A refrigerator installer will charge extra for hooking up a water line to an automatic ice cube maker. Since you are already paying for this service, your tip, if given, should reflect his overall work and not be based on something you may think is an extra effort on his part but which is actually being billed to you anyway.

When a delivery or installation comes at a time that you don't have cash on hand to give a tip, business owners tell me that it is not uncommon to add an extra amount to the payment of the bill for the purchase with a notation that it is to be given to the delivery or installation personnel as you designate.

Q. How can I "tip" people who provide care or service to me and my family when it would be inappropriate to give them money? I am thinking of such people as my children's teachers, the person who is especially helpful at our local clothing store, and the salesman at the carpet store who gave me such good advice.

A. You can always remember these people with a small gift during the holidays, at the end of the school year, or after the completion of work, such as the installation of your carpeting after the planning you did with the salesman. Remember, however, that passing on your thanks, praise, and commendation not only to the person but to his or her supervisor is the very nicest way of all to say thank you.

Index

Acceptance of invitations
    after declining, 126
    formal, 121–22
    less formal, 124–25
Acknowledgement of
        gift, lack of,
        154–55
Address, forms of, 32–38
    professional women,
        36
    in telephone calls,
        49–50
        business calls, 52–53
    waiters, 94
Addressing of wedding
        presents, 152
Adoption of child
    announcement of,
        136–37
    baby shower for, 137
Advance time for invita-
        tions, 121
Advice, unwanted, 10–11
Affection, public dis-
        plays of, 8–9, 15

Age, questions about,
        39
AIDS, 9
Airplane personnel, and
        tips, 165
À la carte, 91–92
Animals. *See* Pets
Anniversary
    gifts, thank-you notes
        and, 156
    invitations, 140
    party, 140
Announcements
    of adoption of child,
        136–37
    of birth of child,
        135–36
    of engagement, 131–32
    of graduation, 141–42
    of name change, 49
    of wedding, 128–30
Answer cards, 126–27
Answering services, 171
Answering of telephone,
        49

Apartment living guidelines, 14

Arrival time, at dinner party, 27
late-arriving guests, 27–28

At home cards, 134

Au pair, tip for, 171

Baby gifts, brought to hospital, 158

Baby shower, 133
for adopted child, 137

Baby sitter, tips for, 171–72

Barber, tip for, 172

Bar mitzvah invitations, 61

Bar steward, tip for, 166

Bartender, tip for, 161

Bath steward, tip for, 166

Beach attire, 15

Beach behavior, 14–15

Beauty salon, tipping, 172–73

Bellman/bellwoman, tip for, 167

Beverages
cold, 86
hot, 85–86
see also Glasses

Birth announcements, 135–36

Birthday gifts
to business associates, 64–65

children and, 145–46
thank-you notes for, 156

Birthday parties
for adults, 143–44
for children, 144–46

Blind people, behavior with, 21–22

Blowing nose, at table, 87–88

Boss, invitations to, 60

Bread
and butter, to eat, 85
uncut, in restaurant, 93

Bridal showers, for older couples, 152–53

Brit, invitation to, 138–39

Building superintendent, Christmas tip for, 177

Burial, attendance at, 115

Busboys, tip for, 161

Business associates:
addressing, 56
dinner in home of, 62–63
first-name use, 34
funerals of, 119
paying for lunch with, 60
wedding invitations to, 61

Business cards, 59

Business entertaining
greeting guests, 52–63

role of spouse in, 62
Bus tours, tipping and, 165
Butcher, tip for, 173
Butter knife
  formal place setting, 70
  informal place setting, 72
Butter plate
  family-style setting, 69, 74
  formal place setting, 69
  informal place setting, 72

Cabin boy, tip for, 166
Cabin steward, tip for, 165
Cafeteria-style restaurant, 97–99
Call waiting, 53–54
Candles, 71
Car pools, 66
Caterers, tip for, 161
Chain letters, 48–49
Chambermaid, tip for, 167–68
Champagne glasses, 78
Charter bus, tipping on, 165
Checkroom attendant, tip for, 162
Children
  addressing correspondence to, 46–47

addressing friends of parents, 11
adoption announcement, 136–37
and adults-only visit, 22–23
friends of, 12
godparents and, 139
inclusion in invitations, 128
offering of seat, 8
preparing for visit from, 23
shaking hands with, 40
sharing of toys, 15–16
stepchildren, 2–3
Choking on food, 87
Christening
  invitation to, 138
  outfit, 140
Christmas cards, 47–48
  appropriate messages in, 47
  children's names on, 47
  printed, 47–48
Christmas gifts
  thank-you notes and, 156
  unexpected, 148–49
Christmas greetings, 25
Churches, 100–105
  appropriate dress for, 101–2
  change of, 103

Churches (*cont.*)
noisy or rude behavior
in, 103–5
participation in, outside
affiliation and, 105
Client, entertained by
sales rep, 159
Clothing
beach attire, 15
christening outfit, 140
for funerals, 115
for weddings, 133–34
for worship services,
101–2
Coat, checked at restau-
rant, 89
Coffee cups, 75
Commercial messenger,
tip for, 173
Communications
e-mail letters, 43–44
faxed, 43
see also Correspon-
dence
Condiments, family-style
meals and, 74
Condolence calls, 106–7
Condolence notes, 112
thank-you notes for,
156
Condolences, response
to, 119
Congratulatory cards or
gifts, and thank-
you notes, 156

Correspondence
business, 58–59
to couple with differ-
ent names, 44
e-mail, 43–44
salutation when
name/sex is
unknown, 45
typed personal letters,
44
Coughing, at table, 87–88
Couples
public displays of
affection, 8–9
in restaurants, 90, 91
Cruise director, 166
Cruise ships, tipping
guidelines for,
165–67

Dairy delivery, tipping,
173
Dating etiquette, 6
Deaf people, behavior
with, 20–21
Deaths
condolence calls, 106–7
newspaper notices,
107–9, 113
notification of rela-
tives, 107
role of friends follow-
ing, 110–11
Declining of invitation
after acceptance, 126

enclosing note with regrets, 127
formal, 122
less formal, 123–24
Delivery people, tips for, 173–74, 179
Desk clerk, 168
Dessert, how to eat, 83–84
Dessert spoon/fork
formal table setting, 71
informal table setting, 72
Diaper service, tipping, 174
Dining steward, tip for, 165
Dinner guest
late-arriving, 27
refusal of dish, 81
request for missing item, 80
Dinner knife, table setting
family-style, 73, 74
informal, 72
Dinner parties
arrival times, 27
thank-you notes, 156
Dinner plate, table setting
family-style, 75
informal, 73
Divorce, announcement of, 3–4

Divorced persons
and family occasions, 1–2
and funeral of ex-spouse, 113
new relationships and, 2
woman, form of name, 4
Doctors, addressing correspondence to, 46
Doggy bags, 95
Dog walkers, 17–18
Door attendant, tip for, 168
Door person, Christmas tip, 177
Drunken guests, 30
Dry cleaner, tip for, 173

Elevator operators, 177
Elevators, 8
E-mail letters, 43–44
Engagement
announcement of, 131–32
broken, and return of gifts, 150
Engagement party, 131
England, tipping in, 178–79
Engraved engagement announcements, 132

Ethnic slurs, 19
Europe, tipping in,
     178–79
Ex-family members,
     introduction of, 36

Facsimiles, private, 43
Farewell party, 142–43
Fish fork, 70
Fish knife, 70
Florist, tipping, 174
Flowers
  for hosts, 149
  "in lieu of flowers,"
     109
Food
  choking on, 87–88
  excess, in restaurants,
     95
  foreign object in, 88
  as gift to host, 149–50
  stuck in tooth, 88
Foreign object, in food,
     88
Forks
  family-style table set-
     tings, 73, 74
  formal table settings,
     69, 70
  informal table settings,
     72
  proper use of, 82
Friendship, mixing with
     business, 63–64
Frozen dinners, 74

Fruit spoon, 70
Funeral
  appropriate clothing
     for, 115
  attendance, 112–13,
     115, 119
  ushers, 111–12
Funeral home visits,
     112–14
Furniture deliverers, 176

Garage valet, tip for, 168
Garbage collectors, tip-
     ping, 174
Gift certificates, 147
Gift collections, in office,
     64–65
Gifts
  arrived broken, 150–51
  for children, at birth-
     day parties,
     144–46
  duplicate, 145
  engagement, 150
  for host/hostess,
     149–50, 158
  money as, 147
  monogrammed, 153
  "no gift" requests, 142,
     147–48
  opening at party, 148
  questions on cost of, 39
  "real" vs. "gag", 144
  returned, on broken
     engagement, 150

unacknowledged,
154–55
unexpected, 148–49
wedding, 150, 151, 152,
158
Glasses
champagne, 78
family-style table set-
ting, 74
formal table setting, 69
informal table setting,
72
wineglasses, 77–79
Godparents, 139
Golf caddies, 170
Good host/hostess, 27
Good neighbor, 13–14
Grace, before meal,
75–76
Graduation announce-
ments, 141–42
Gravy, 80
Greeting cards, hand-
delivered, 48
Greetings
before worship service,
103
in restaurants, 94–95
Grief, times of, 106–19
Grocery loaders, 174
Guardians, 139
Guests
asking to leave, 31
asking to remove
shoes, 26–27

discouraging from
mixing drinks in
home, 29
greeting at door, 62
inebriated, 30
late-arriving, 27–28
starting to eat, 76–77
unexpected, 22–23,
23–24

Hair, arrangement of, in
restaurants, 94
Handicapped people,
behavior with,
19–22
Handshakes, 40
Handwritten invitations,
123
response to, 125
Hats, in worship service,
102
Headwaiter, tip for, 97,
162–63, 168–69
Health club personnel,
170–71
Hearing disabled people,
behavior with,
20–21
Holidays
Christmas tipping
guidelines, 171–78
divorced parents and,
1–2
greeting people of dif-
ferent faiths, 25

Honorary pallbearers, 111

Hospital
  gifts for staff, 174–75
  visits, 22

Host/hostess
  gifts for, 149–59
  hallmarks of good, 27
  offer of assistance to, 31
  of restaurant dinner, 96–97
  rising to feet, 41

Housecleaners, tipping, 175

Household helpers, tipping, 175

Houses of worship, 100–105

Housewarming party, 142

Identification of telephone caller, 49–50

Inebriated guests, 30

In lieu of flowers, 109–10

Instructor, tip for, 170

Introductions, 32–38
  forgotten names, 36–37
  incorrect, 39
  of live-in partners, 35
  response to, 37–38
  of stepparents, 35–36

Invitations, 120–30
  advance time, 121
  anniversary, 140
  to business associates, 60–63
  christening or *brit*, 138–39
  formal third-person, 120–21
  printed, 124
  by telephone, 125
  see also Response to invitation

Janitor, Christmas tip for, 177

Jewish families, condolence calls on, 106

Job. *See* Work environment

Knives
  family-style meals, 73, 74
  formal place settings, 70, 71
  informal place settings, 72
  proper use of, 82–83

"Ladies first" rule, 7

Late-arriving guests, 27

Laundry service, tipping, 176

Leaving parties, 28–29

Letter carriers, 176

Linens
bedding, 26
table, 71
Lipstick, use of, 68, 94
Live-in child care, tips
for, 171–72
Live-together relation-
ships, 4–5
introductions and, 5,
35
Locker-room attendant,
tip for, 170
Loss, times of, 106–19
Lounge steward, tip for,
166
Luggage porters, 169–70
Lunch invitation, to boss,
60

Maiden name, used after
marriage, 45
Married women
business correspon-
dence and, 59
signature of, 44–45, 59
Masseur, tip for, 170
Meat fork, formal place
setting, 70
Meat knife
formal place setting, 70
informal place setting,
72
Memorial service,
116–17. *See also*
Funeral

Men
dress for weddings,
133–34
handshakes, 30
introduced to women,
32
offering of seat, 8
rising to feet, 40, 95
walking with women,
6–7
Money gifts, 147
Monogrammed gifts, 153
Motel personnel, 167–69
Movers, 176
Mugs, for hot beverages,
85–86
Musicians, tipping, 163

Names
changes of, 49
forgotten, 36–37
maiden name, used
after marriage, 134
mispronounced, 39–40
suffixes, 12
Napkin rings, 74
Napkins
family-style setting, 75
formal table setting, 70
informal, 72
proper way of han-
dling, 76
Neighborliness, 13–14
Newlyweds, names for
spouses' parents, 11

Newspaper announcements
 death notices, 107–9, 113
 of engagement, 131–32
Newspaper carriers, tipping, 176

Obituaries, 109
Obscene telephone calls, 52
Offensive forms of address, 58
Office environment. See Work environment
Oriental restaurant, 97, 98–99
Over-the-hill gifts, 144
Overnight visits
 bedding and, 26
 thank-you notes, 156
Oyster fork, 70

Pallbearers, 111, 119
Parking service, tip for, 168, 176–77
Parties, leaving, 28–29
Passing dishes at table, 80
Passover Seder, 100–101
Pastor, addressing correspondence to, 46
Pets
 objection to, 13, 17–18
 taking on visits, 18

Physically disabled people, behavior with, 19–22
Porter, tip for, 166
Posture, at dinner table, 69
Prayer, before meal, 75–76
Prejudice, in social situations, 38–39
Priest, asking blessing of, 100
Printed invitations, 124
Private duty nurses, 175
Public behavior, 14–15
Public displays of affection, 8–9, 15

Reaching, at table, 79–80
Reaffirmation of wedding vows, 141
Receiving line, after memorial service, 116–17
Reception, after funeral/memorial service, 117–18
Red wine, 78
Refusing a dish, 81
Religion, showing respect for others', 25–26, 101
Reservations, in restaurants, 89

Residential building
employees,
Christmas tips for,
177
Response to invitation
change of, 126
formal, 121
timing of, 128
Restaurants
cafeteria-style, 97–99
giving order in, 92
greeting friends in,
94–95
hosting dinner in,
96–97
oriental, 97–99
reservations in, 89
smorgasbord, 97–99
summoning waiter in,
94
table manners in,
92–94
Retirement parties, 143
Rising to feet, 40–41, 95
Room waiter, tip for, 169

Salad, how to eat, 85
Salad fork
family-style setting, 74
formal place setting,
69–70
informal place setting,
72
Salad knife, formal place
setting, 70

Salt
passing, 80
in saltcellar, 86–87
Salutation of letter
on business letter,
58–59
when name/sex is
unknown, 45
Service plates, 69, 72
Sexually transmitted
disease, 9–10
Sherry glass, 79
Ship's officers, 166
Shoes, asking guests to
remove, 26–27
Shoeshines, 177
Shower gifts, 156
Showers
baby, 133, 137–38
bridal, 132–33
Sick person
gifts to, 156
visits to, 22
Sitting *shivah*, 106
Sleeping car porters, 170
Smoking, 16–17
Smorgasbord restaurant,
97–99
Sneezing, at table, 87–88
Socializing, for business,
57–58
business dinners, in
private home,
62–63
return invitations, 62

Socializing, for business (*cont.*)
    spouse's role, in business entertaining, 62
Soup, serving and eating, 84
Soup spoon
    formal place setting, 70
    informal place setting, 72
Spills, at table, 88–89
Sports club personnel, 170–71
Spouse
    invitation from business associate, 60–61
    name for parents of, 11
    role in business entertaining, 62
Standing up, 40–41, 95
Stepchildren, 2–3
Stepparents, introducing, 35–36
Stranger, conversation with, 38
Suffix, after name, 12
Sympathy
    acknowledgment of, 118–19
    expressions of, 106–7
Synagogue, appropriate dress for, 101–2

Table d'hôte, 91
Table linens, 71
Table manners, 67–68, 76–77, 79–89
    dos and don'ts, 67–68
    choosing flatware, 81
    handling napkin, 76
    passing salt/pepper, 80
    prayer, before meal, 75–76
    reaching, at table, 79–80
    refusing a dish, 81
    in restaurant, 92–94
Table settings, 68–75
    family-style, 73–75
    formal, 69–71
    informal, 71–73
Tactless people, 38–39
Taxi drivers, tipping, 169
Tea bags, 86
Telephone calls
    answering, 49
    caller giving name immediately, 49–50
    forwarding, 54
    invitations, 50–51
    obscene, 52
    response to invitations, 50–51
    wrong numbers, 51–52
Telephone manners, 49–50

gift collections in, 64–65
host/hostess gifts, 62–63
importance of courtesy, 55
invitations, 60–63
kissing in, 57
offensive forms of address, 58
personal hygiene in, 65–66
salutation on business letter, 58–59

seating, at meetings, 56
telephone manners, 52–53, 59–60
traveling with boss, 55–56
see also Business entertaining
Wrong telephone numbers, 51–52

Yarmulkes, 102
Young person, introduced to older person, 32

About the Author

Elizabeth L. Post, granddaughter-in-law of the legendary Emily Post, has earned the mantle of her predecessor as America's foremost authority on etiquette. Mrs. Post has revised the classic *Etiquette* five times since 1965. In addition, she has written *Emily Post's Complete Book of Wedding Etiquette; Emily Post's Wedding Planner; Emily Post's Advice for Every Dining Occasion; Emily Post on Business Etiquette; Emily Post on Entertaining; Emily Post on Guests and Hosts; Emily Post on Invitations; Emily Post on Second Weddings; Emily Post on Weddings; Please, Say Please; The Complete Book of Entertaining* with co-author Anthony Staffieri; and *Emily Post's Teen Etiquette* with co-author Joan M. Coles. Mrs. Post's advice on etiquette may also be found in the monthly column she writes for *Good Housekeeping* magazine, "Etiquette for Everyday."

Besides the books she has written, Mrs. Post's work is now featured in her first multimedia product: *Emily Post's Complete Guide to Weddings,* available on CD-ROM for Windows™.

Mrs. Post and her husband divide their time between homes in Florida and Vermont.

business versus social, 52–53
call waiting, 53–54
during personal visits, 53
Temperature for serving wine, 77–78
Thank-you notes, 154
baby gifts, after birth, 158
not received, 154–55
obligatory, 156, 158
optional or unnecessary, 157, 159
timing of, 154
for wedding gifts, 155
Tipping, 160–80
calculating, 178
guidelines, 160
of headwaiter, 97, 162–63
at health or sports clubs, 170–71
in hotels/full service motels, 167–69
personal and professional services, 171–78
in restaurants, 161–64
taxi drivers, 169
when traveling, 165–70
Train travel, tipping guidelines for, 169–70
Typed personal letters, 44

Unacknowledged gifts, 154–55
Unexpected gifts, 148–49
Unexpected guests, 22–23, 23–24
Unmarried couples
live-together relationships, 4–5, 35
wedding invitations to, 128
Unwanted advice, 10–11
Ushers
in church, 102
at funerals, 111–12, 119
tipping, 177–78

Valets, 169
Visitors, included in invitations, 125–26
Visits
from children, 23
of condolence, 106–7
in funeral home, 112
hospital, 22
overnight, 26
pets and, 18
unexpected guests, 22–23, 23–24
Volunteer services, 24–25

Waiter/waitress
complaints/compliments to, 96
room waiter, 169
summoning, 94

Waiter/waitress (*cont.*)
tip for, 163–64, 168,
169
Walking, in couples, 6–7
Washroom attendant,
164
Water goblet, 78
informal place setting,
72
Wedding announcement,
128–29
expense of, 130
Wedding gifts
duplicate, 151
money as, 147
return of, 150,
151
thank-you notes for,
158
when and where deliv-
ered, 152
whom to address to,
152
wedding invitations
advance time, 121
to business associates,
61
to guests of unmarried
persons, 131
response cards, 127
Wedding showers,
132–33
Whispering, 25
Wine, temperature for
serving, 77–78

Wineglasses
formal place setting,
69, 71
informal place setting,
72, 73
Wine steward, tip for,
164, 166
Women
divorced, and form of
name, 4
dress for formal wed-
dings, 133
dress for informal
weddings, 134
dress for semiformal
weddings, 133
and handshakes, 40
names in death notices,
108
ordering in restaurant,
91
professional, form of
address for, 36
rising to feet, 40–41
walking with men, 6–7
widowed, and form of
name, 4
Work environment,
55–66
addressing coworkers,
56
after-hours socializing,
57–58, 62–63
business lunches, 60
car pools, 66